INFLUENTIAL
L!VES

KEVIN HART

Comedian, Actor, Writer, and Producer

Susan Kauffman

 Enslow Publishing
101 W. 23rd Street
Suite 240
New York, NY 10011
USA

enslow.com

Published in 2018 by Enslow Publishing, LLC.
101 W. 23rd Street, Suite 240, New York, NY 10011

Library of Congress Cataloging-in-Publication Data

Names: Kauffman, Susan.
Title: Kevin Hart: comedian, actor, writer, and producer / Susan Kauffman.
Description: New York : Enslow Publishing, 2018 | Series: Influential lives | Includes index and bibliography. | Audience: Grades 6-12.
Identifiers: ISBN 9780766085077 (library bound)
Subjects: LCSH: Hart, Kevin, 1979-. | Comedians--United States--Biography--Juvenile literature. | African American comedians--Biography--Juvenile literature. | Actors--United States--Biography--Juvenile literature. | African American actors--Biography--Juvenile literature.
Classification: LCC PN2287.H368 K38 2018 | DDC 792.702/8092--dc23

Printed in the United States of America

To Our Readers: We have done our best to make sure all websites in this book were active and appropriate when we went to press. However, the author and the publisher have no control over and assume no liability for the material available on those websites or on any websites they may link to. Any comments or suggestions can be sent by e-mail to customerservice@enslow.com.

Photo credits: Cover, p. 1 Jason Merritt/Getty Images; p. 4 © AMC Theatres; p. 7 John D. Kisch/Separate Cinema Archive/Moviepix/Getty Images; pp. 14, 41 Featureflash Photo Agency/Shutterstock.com; p. 16 Wally McNamee/Corbis/Getty Images; p. 18 Everett Collection, Inc./Alamy Stock Photo; p. 21 Maury Phillips Archive/WireImage/Getty Images; p. 25 Michael Buckner/Getty Images; p. 31 Lyle A. Waisman/WireImage/Getty Images; pp. 36, 45 © AP Images; p. 49 Earl Gibson III/WireImage/Getty Images; p. 52 Gilbert Carrasquillo/WireImage/Getty Images; p. 54 AF archive/Alamy Stock Photo; p. 57 Jeff Fusco/Getty Images; p. 62 Kevin Mazur/KCA2014/WireImage/Getty Images; p. 66 WENN Ltd/Alamy Stock Photo; pp. 68, 82–83 Atlaspix/Alamy Stock Photo; p. 71 MediaPunch Inc/Alamy Stock Photo; p. 74 ZUMA Press, Inc./Alamy Stock Photo; p. 78 Michael Tran/FilmMagic/Getty Images; p. 87 Kevin Winter/Getty Images; pp. 90–91 Albert L. Ortega/Getty Images; p. 98 Jason LaVeris/FilmMagic/Getty Images; back cover and interior pages background graphic zffoto/Shutterstock.com.

Contents

Chapter One

Keeping It Real

• •

R ising on a small platform elevator from beneath the stage, Kevin Hart is about to make history. He steps onto the stage, casually dressed in a grey jacket, T-shirt, jeans, and tennis shoes, ready to perform his Laugh at My Pain routine to an audience of fifteen thousand, many of whom are well-known celebrities. Hart visited ninety cities on his international Laugh at My Pain stand-up tour, and his two-night performance at L.A. Live's Nokia Theatre (now known as the Microsoft Theater) sold out. It was one of the most successful comedy tours in history.

The theatrical version of *Laugh at My Pain*, which was released in September 2011, begins with a documentary of Hart visiting his hometown of North Philadelphia; it then switches over to a one-hour live performance at the Nokia Theatre. In his act, Hart

• • • • • • • • • • • • • • • • • •

Kevin Hart showcased his energy, enthusiasm, and personal life stories in the documentary *Laugh at My Pain*. This unusual venture made him one of the most popular comedians in the country.

What Is *The Original Kings of Comedy*?

The Original Kings of Comedy is a stand-up comedy concert film released in 2000 featuring four well-known African American comedians: Steve Harvey, D. L. Hughley, Cedric the Entertainer, and Bernie Mac. The concert, filmed live at the Charlotte Coliseum in Charlotte, North Carolina, was directed by Spike Lee, a film director, writer, producer, and actor. The four different comedy styles of the Kings "create options for viewers, so if you don't like one of them, you'll like someone else."[1] The Kings also give the audience a chance to see them behind the scenes, hanging out backstage, playing cards, and playing basketball. The movie inspired spin-offs such as *The Queens of Comedy* and *The Comedians of Comedy*. It was nominated for the 2001 National Association for the Advancement of Colored People (NAACP) Image Award and the 2001 Chicago Film Critics Association Award.

pokes fun at his personal life, from his rough childhood to his mother's funeral, and he uses pyrotechnics as a spotlight for his punch lines. The movie grossed more than $7 million and became 2011's most successful film of those released in fewer than three hundred theaters.

Not only did Laugh at My Pain become one of the most successful comedy tours in history but it also placed Kevin Hart on the same list as other well-known

The Original Kings of Comedy—left to right, Bernie Mac, Cedric the Entertainer, D. L. Hughley, and Steve Harvey—made audiences laugh with their views about African American culture, race relations, religion, and family.

comedians, including Richard Pryor, Eddie Murphy, and the "Original Kings of Comedy." This was a big step for him. As he admitted, "At the end of the day, I want to be part of the same conversation as Chris Rock, Eddie Murphy, Dave Chappelle, Bill Cosby and Richard Pryor."[2] One of the Original Kings, Steve Harvey, a comedian and talk show host who has been an advisor to Hart for several years, says that Hart understands how to gain an audience's attention. Harvey explains that Hart "is willing to share his life and experiences from his past. He is open about his relationship, his parenting skills and his childhood."[3]

"I came, I saw, I rocked!"[4]

Hart never planned to be an entertainer, at least not as a comedian. And it never crossed his mind that he would become one of the most famous comedians in history. When he was young and living in a one-bedroom apartment with his mom and brother, he hoped to one day have a better life, maybe a bigger house and a nice car. Then he started doing stand-up comedy, receiving advice from seasoned comedians. He realized that, if he worked hard enough, his dreams of a nicer life might come true. Now, up onstage, in front of thousands of people, he knows the dream is coming true.

Living in a rough neighborhood with a dad who was a drug addict and a mom who raised him on her own is

How to Make It as a Comedian

According to five of New York City's best comedy writers, an important piece of advice for beginning comedians is to start honing their skills immediately. Comedians should prepare by writing jokes and developing their own voice so that they are ready when that big break comes along. Beginning comedians also shouldn't let their role models influence them. They should use their own voice, not mimic others. To stay "in the game," comedians should broaden their careers, whether writing a comedy novel or acting in a comedy film. Something both beginning and seasoned comedians need is luck to place them in the right place at the right time. And last, but not necessarily least, a comedian needs to be ready for rejection. Comedians at the beginning of their careers as well as seasoned comedians are prone to rejection; it shouldn't be taken personally.[5]

actually what makes Kevin Hart the man he is today. He talks about his father "and the difficulties of dealing with this at a young age. I let you see it first-hand . . . These aren't stories that are fabricated or staged to be funny."[6] And when the audience understands that the jokes Hart delivers aren't made-up stories, that they are real, and that the comedian is just like them, they relate to him. They see Kevin Hart as regular guy who grew up with a caring family but with many bumps along the way. They see that he is real.

The fact that Hart is loud and rambunctious helps in his comedy routines as well. He has a different style of comedy. He gets physical—swaggering across the stage, playing with the microphone, falling on the floor to mimic friends, and using theatrics to entertain his audience. He is able to control his crowd, even in sold-out arenas that seat tens of thousands of people. He can be loud, easily changing his voice from high pitched to gruff. Then he becomes quiet, somehow managing to get his audience to stop laughing and to listen to him. Hart has no problem putting himself out there—every part of him—for the world to see. He wants his fans to feel like he is one of them, like their lovable, funny neighbor.

"**Everybody wants to be famous, but no one wants to do the work.**"[7]

Kevin Hart is real. He is lovable. He is hilarious. And he is about to take comedy to a whole new level.

CHAPTER TWO

Finding Himself

• •

K evin Darnell Hart was born on July 6, 1979, in Philadelphia, Pennsylvania. His neighborhood of North Philadelphia was known as one of the rougher neighborhoods in the city, where acts of violence were reaching record-breaking numbers in the early 1990s, when Kevin would have been reaching his teens. Resources for education, jobs, and youth activities were suffering. Many teenagers and young adults felt like they didn't have much of a future, which led them to the streets, crime, and drugs. But rather than turn to the streets, Kevin became involved in extracurricular activities, including swimming with the Philadelphia Department of Recreation (PDR) swim team at the Salvation Army KROC center and playing basketball for George Washington High School's varsity basketball team.

Troubled Family Life

Taking part in school and after-school activities helped Kevin move in a different direction than

> "You need to learn to apply yourself ... not hang with kids who only bring each other down.[1]"

other teenagers in his neighborhood, but Kevin credits a large part of his growing up with the right attitude to his mom, Nancy Hart. Most important to Nancy was a good education. She relocated from Florida to Philadelphia to attend college and earned a BA in commerce and engineering from Drexel University.

Pride, Determination, Resilience

In 2007, *Pride*, a biographical film based on Kevin Hart's swim coach James Ellis, was released. *Pride* told the story of Ellis's efforts to rehabilitate an old pool at the Marcus Foster Recreation Center and to create Philadelphia's first all-African American swim team. By 1990, Ellis created the largest group of black swimmers to compete at the Junior National Championship. Three of the PDR swimmers had times that placed them among the top six in their events nationally, and eight others ranked in the regional top ten. Because of Ellis's efforts, swimmers from Marcus Foster have taken part in the swimming trials for every US Olympic team since 1992. Ellis received the President's Award from the International Swimming Hall of Fame "for his accomplishments as a coach and mentor, as well as for bringing his personal story to the Big Screen."[2]

Kevin, however, wasn't too interested in school. He was a mediocre student and was known as the class clown. Kevin had his own dreams. He wanted to play basketball professionally. Even when he realized that his growth spurt stopped in fourth grade at five feet four inches, Kevin still had hope. "In my mind, I was still the tallest kid in the fourth grade," he explains. "I think I might have technically been the same height from fourth grade to eighth grade. But I refused to acknowledge it."[3]

Nancy raised Kevin and his brother, Robert, who is eight years older than Kevin, on her own while working full-time as a computer analyst at the University of Pennsylvania. They lived in a small one-bedroom row house in North Philadelphia; Kevin and Robert's bedroom was a

> **"The reason I am the way I am is because my mom was strong.[5]"**

bunk bed in the hallway. When Kevin was young, his dad, Henry Witherspoon, had a problem with drugs. He wasn't around often, but when he was, he did what he could to help out. Robert, who became somewhat of a father figure to Kevin, tried to hide his father's actions from Kevin. He explains, "Kevin was too young to know" how "dysfunctional . . . it was."[4]

There were times, however, when Kevin's brother wasn't around to hide him from their dad's behavior. And those are the times that he most often jokes about onstage today when talking about his dad. He will even tell his audience that the stories are true and that there

Although his father was in and out of his life for most of Hart's childhood, he was proud to share a moment of stardom with his dad, along with his brother, Robert, and actress Halle Berry.

is no way he could make them up. He often pokes fun at the time his dad showed up at one of his spelling bees. Witherspoon was high on drugs and treated the spelling bees like a sporting event. There were also times when Witherspoon would share with Kevin some of the things he was willing to do to get drugs—things that young children wouldn't typically hear from their dad.

When Kevin was a little older, hitting his teenage years, he was out with his dad one day when his dad pointed to another young man and told Kevin that was his brother. Kevin, who only knew Robert as his brother, didn't comprehend what his dad meant at first. He later realized that his dad had three sons; the one he pointed to was his dad's son with another woman.

Eventually, Witherspoon's drug addiction turned chronic. He was using heroin, crack, and cocaine and had spent time in jail. It reached a point that nothing but drugs mattered to him. He didn't even see the negativity in stealing twenty dollars from Kevin's birthday money. When Kevin was eight years old, his mother kicked Witherspoon out of the house. After that, he was in and out of Kevin's life throughout the rest of his childhood.

The Seeds of Comedy

Kevin began to rely on his humor to deal with his family life and his small size. He was the class clown, which made him popular with his classmates and kept him from being picked on because of his size. And although Robert often didn't find Kevin's antics too funny, explaining that Kevin was "my younger brother so he wasn't funny to me, he was stupid," Kevin was a hit at family gatherings.[6]

Like Hart, Eddie Murphy learned early in life that he was a natural comedian. Murphy's first stand-up comedy album, *Delirious*, influenced up-and-coming comedians such as Dave Chappelle, Chris Rock, and, of course, Kevin Hart.

• •

According to Hart, he was about ten years old when he first realized that he was really funny. He had his family in tears from laughter at a family reunion when he started doing impressions of his mom and aunts. But the thought of being a stand-up comedian never crossed his mind.

Nancy wouldn't allow Kevin and Robert to watch anything on television that was rated R or that had bad language. So it wasn't until Kevin was fifteen years old that he saw Eddie Murphy's stand-up television comedy

Eddie Murphy: Comedian

Eddie Murphy was raised by his mom after his dad died when Eddie was three years old. When Eddie was eight years old, his mom became ill, so Eddie and his older brother were placed into foster care for one year, where Eddie developed his sense of humor. By the time Eddie was fifteen years old, he was writing and performing his own routines.

His career started to take off when he became a regular cast member of *Saturday Night Live*. *Delirious*, originally a television comedy special, was Murphy's first stand-up film. Released as an album titled *Eddie Murphy: Comedian*, it won Best Comedy Album at the 1984 Grammy Awards. His second stand-up comedy film, *Eddie Murphy Raw*, grossed $50.5 million, ranking it the No. 1 box office stand-up film of all time. Murphy is ranked No. 10 on Comedy Central's 100 Greatest Stand-ups of All Time.

special *Delirious*. "I was just in awe of the presence that he had. He commanded your attention the minute he walked out," he explains.[7] Little did Kevin know that he would one day be compared to Eddie Murphy.

Kevin graduated from the George Washington High School in 1997 with a C average. His mom was adamant that he continue his education, so he attended the Community College of Philadelphia as a theater major. After a short stint in college, Kevin decided college wasn't for him, and he dropped out.

The Funniest Man's Funniest Film

RICHARD PRYOR
LIVE IN CONCERT

Before Eddie Murphy, there was Richard Pryor, often considered the gold standard by other comedians. His *Live in Concert* was the first full-length movie of purely stand-up comedy.

Lil' Kev

He started working as a shoe salesman at City Sports in Philadelphia. Like the class clown he was in school, Hart was the funny guy at work. When it was slow, he would entertain his coworkers with his sense of humor. "When you provide a good time to people without being forced," Hart explains, "it shows that you're naturally funny."[8] His coworkers talked him into trying out his skills onstage. The Laff House Comedy Club in Philadelphia held an amateur comedian night every Thursday. The Laff House was one of the few places dedicated to Philadelphia's comedy scene; it has been a shrine to Philadelphia's comedians for more than twenty years. The club gave comedy newbies, particularly black comedians, a place to show off their talents. It represents the place where many well-known comedians, including Chris Rock, TuRae, and Michael Blackson, got their start. In 2013, the original Laff House closed after one of its owners, Mona Millwood, passed away. After recovering from the loss of his wife, Rod Millwood decided that he needed to bring back the Laff House—"a place for people who had no place to go, but were funny."[9]

Hart agreed to try it out and had one week to prepare. He spent the week practicing jokes that related to his commute to and from work, and he used the stage name Lil' Kev. There were about seventeen people in the audience that night, six of whom were his coworkers. At age nineteen, this was a big deal for Hart. Unfortunately, he bombed and was booed off the stage.

But Hart didn't let his first failed attempt at stand-up comedy break him. He actually loved it and couldn't wait to get back onstage. Hart describes that he "walked off feeling like if I were to really study this and understand this, I could do it."[10] For the next six weeks, he returned every Thursday night to perform. In his first few performances, he would imitate other comedians who influenced him. Keith Robinson, a veteran comedian, watched as Hart failed his first performance but was more accepted by the audience in his second, although Robinson thought Kevin's first show was better because he was more himself.

Robinson saw something in Hart and decided to mentor him, with his first piece of advice being that Hart should use his own voice. "The material that's going to take you farther is the material that's drawn from you," explained Robinson. "But it's better to struggle with your stuff than do the stuff everybody is doing."[11] From that advice, Hart began to bring his personal life and his short stature into his acts. He basically belittled himself and his life onstage; the audience loved it. And as for Hart, poking fun at his personal life, such as his dad's drug habits and his rough childhood, became his therapy for coping with his difficult childhood.

Robinson started finding additional opportunities for Hart to perform in other cities. They would drive to New York City or Atlantic City to perform and then drive home the same night. Hart didn't make much more than twenty-five dollars for a show, but he gained a lot of experience as well as advice. Once at the Comedy Cellar in New York City, Hart underwent a comedic ritual called Hack Court. Hack Court is a comedy court where veteran comedians judge the jokes of beginning

Hart and his first wife, Torrei, had plans to make it big in Hollywood. Together, they moved to California to pursue their dreams and quickly started rising to stardom: Kevin as a famous comedian and actor and Torrei as an actress and producer.

comedians. Robinson and a group of other seasoned comedians who watched Hart perform that night took him into a back room and put him "on trial for his crimes against comedy."[12] They told Hart that one of his favorite jokes, and what he thought was one of his best, "stunk" and that Hart should forget it.

During a club performance at Sweet Cheeks in Atlantic City, an audience member threw a buffalo wing at Hart. He explained that he tried to stand up to the person who threw it. "'Whoever threw it, say you threw it so I can see you.' And this guy actually stood up, and I was like, 'All right, never mind, good night everybody.' He was big."[13]

The Value of a Support Network

Hart was fortunate enough to have a lot of support while he worked on his career. On the road, he had Robinson and other veteran comedians to teach him the ins and outs of comedy. And at home, he had two very important people who stood by his side—his then girlfriend, Torrei, and his mom.

Throughout his early years in the small comedy clubs of Philadelphia to his early movie appearances, Torrei was there to support him. Kevin and Torrei met while attending the Community College of Philadelphia. Together they moved to Los Angeles to pursue their careers in entertainment. They had a low-profile wedding in 2003, and two years later, Torrei gave birth to their first child, Heaven Leigh. Their second child, Hendrix, was born three years later in November 2008.

Kevin's mom, Nancy, was always there to support him as well. When Hart first decided to quit his job as a shoe salesman to become a full-time comedian, he knew he might need help financially. He asked his mom if she could help him with his rent when he needed it. Although Nancy was skeptical about Kevin's decision, she agreed to support him when needed, but only for one year and as long as he promised to read his Bible. Anytime Kevin would ask his mom for help with his rent, she would ask if he read his Bible. After a few months of this, Kevin finally opened his Bible, only to find several rent checks that his mom had hidden inside.

Nancy stood by Kevin as he worked on his career, from performing in nightclubs to appearing in movies. But she never actually saw him perform. He explains that she didn't like anything about club scenes, such as the smoke and foul language. But Nancy was proud of how hard Kevin was working to make his dreams come true. So, when she was diagnosed with ovarian cancer, she kept it a secret from Kevin for as long as she could because she wanted him to focus on his career. After a long battle with cancer, Nancy Hart died in 2007.

CHAPTER THREE

Growing into "the" Little Man

· · · · · · · · · · · · · · · · ·

In 2000, Robinson introduced Hart to Dave Becky, a talent manager for 3 Arts Entertainment. Becky saw something special in Hart. "He sent me a tape. We get tons of tapes," explained Becky. "I think actually he's the only client I've ever signed off of a tape. Ever."[1] With a handshake deal, Hart and Becky began working together. Not long after, Becky told Kevin that Judd Apatow, a well-known producer of more than twenty movies and nine television shows, wanted Hart to film a pilot for an upcoming television series, *North Hollywood*. For a young comedian still doing acts in comedy clubs, this was a huge opportunity. Hart was given a $25,000 advance that, to him, "felt like $25 million."[2] It is even said that he bought a brand-new Mercedes and told his brother, Robert, that he could stop working. The pilot never aired, but as Hart explained, "My relationship with

Judd Apatow, a well-known producer, writer, director, actor, and comedian, gave Hart his first big break in television. Although the series never aired, Hart and Apatow continued working together to build a great business and personal relationship.

Judd . . . was ultimately more important than anything that could've happened at that time."[3]

First Movie Roles

In addition to building a relationship with Apatow, Hart credits his first appearance at the Montreal Just for Laughs Comedy Festival for his roles in feature films. Appearing at the comedy festival is a great opportunity for young talents to show off their acts in front of entertainment professionals, such as talent

Too Many Roles!

Actors in movies and on television have different titles, or roles, depending on what part they are playing. Understanding the many different roles can be confusing. A lead role—also called a lead actor or star—in a movie plays the largest or most important part in the film. Below the lead actor is the supporting actor. A supporting actor can be a minor or key role that is important to the story, such as a close family member, friend, or sidekick. An actor playing a bit part role interacts with the lead actors but usually has no more than five lines of conversation. Short appearances by well-known celebrities are known as cameo roles or cameo appearances. Many of these roles don't speak. And finally, there are the extras. They usually don't interact with the lead actors nor do they speak, and they are usually uncredited.

scouts, booking agents, and entertainment producers and managers. And, being a young fresh comedian, Hart couldn't pass up this opportunity. Not long after his appearance at the festival, Hart was approached to play the lead role in *Paper Soldiers*. The action comedy, which was Hart's first foray into film, was released in 2002. This debut led to other minor roles in *Scary Movie 3* (2003) and *Scary Movie 4* (2006), *Along Came Polly* (2003), *The 40-Year-Old Virgin* (2005), *Death of a Dynasty* (2003), and *In the Mix* (2005).

Around the same time Hart was working on *Paper Soldiers*, Apatow reached out to him and asked him to appear in the television series *Undeclared*, which Apatow directed and produced. Hart appeared in two episodes in 2002 and another in 2003. The

> "You put me anywhere and I'll shine.[4]"

following year Hart also performed his first televised comedy special on *Comedy Central Presents*. Hart never dreamed that, only a decade later, he would host *Kevin Presents: Keith Robinson*—his first mentor.

Many of the movie roles Hart was receiving were bit roles, but somehow Hart always managed to steal the show. He would get the most memorable lines in the film or bring comedy relief to dramatic moments. Fans were remembering him for these small roles, and even if his name appeared at the bottom of the credits, they wanted to see the movie if for no other reason than to see Kevin Hart.

A Chance at His Own TV Show

Even Hart's small roles were getting him more offers, including one from the ABC network, which offered Kevin his own TV sitcom, *The Big House*. The network flew him to New York to promote the show at the upfronts, an annual weeklong meeting of network executives promoting their shows to advertisers. Literally seconds before he was going onstage to pitch *The Big House*, Hart was told that ABC decided to cancel the show. Six episodes of the show aired on the network in April of that year.

While he was preparing for the sitcom that never was, Hart was busy working on his lead role in the movie *Soul Plane*, alongside comedian Tom Arnold and rapper and actor Snoop Dogg. Unfortunately, the movie bombed. Between this film's failure and the cancellation of *The Big House*, Hart felt like he was "in actor's jail. I couldn't get a job." When asked later if he ever thought his career would continue after playing a lead role in *Soul Plane*, Hart responded that the movie "was supposed to be stupid . . . about a purple plane."[5] Now when Hart talks about his earlier career decisions, he explains, "I'm thankful for the ups and downs in the beginning of my career. They prepare you for what I have now."[6]

Hart continued to make one-episode appearances in television series such as *Love INC* in 2006. And in 2008, he played bit parts in *Drillbit Taylor* and *Extreme Movie*. He also appeared in *Fools Gold*, *Superhero Movie*, and *Meet Dave*, which starred one of his role models, Eddie Murphy.

Going Back to Basics

After some of his acting career setbacks, Hart realized he needed to do more than just make people laugh. That same year, when he was given the opportunity to tour across the country with three other comedians to perform stand-up in large theaters, he turned down the offer. He chose instead to tour on his own at small venues so that he could work on his style.

Comedy Central: Still Going Strong

In the late 1970s and early 1980s, network channels that were devoted to one genre didn't exist (today there are more than five hundred such cable channels). So in the late 1970s, when Art Bell came up with the idea to devote one channel to comedy, he wasn't able to do anything with it. It was almost a decade later before Bell was given the opportunity to pitch his idea to an HBO executive producer, which led to the development of the Comedy Channel.

Launched in November 1989 by HBO, the Comedy Channel was the first cable channel devoted to comedy-based programs. Not long after, MTV launched the comedy channel Ha!, which featured old sitcoms and some short comedy skits. After two years of competition between the two channels, they merged into one—Comedy Central—and today, this network channel entertains more than ninety million households.

This was obviously a good choice because otherwise Hart may not have written, produced, and starred in his first stand-up album, *I'm a Grown Little Man*. In this one-hour Comedy Central special, airing in February 2009, Hart formed a new style of comedy, which was noticeably different from other comedians yet a mixture of many. He is full of energy and always in motion— mimicking, yelling, and pacing back and forth across the stage. Throughout the show, Hart pokes fun at himself, particularly his size; at the beginning of the show, he complains that the microphone is too tall and makes him look small. He even pokes fun at the audience. The special grabbed lots of attention, and people began to view Hart as one of the best young comedy performers. As a result, *I'm a Grown Little Man* became one of the highest-rated specials for Comedy Central.

Shortly before his *I'm a Grown Little Man* special, the film *Not Easily Broken* was released in which Hart played a leading role. The romantic comedy-drama received mixed reviews, but Hart, once again, shone as the comic relief. That same year, he appeared in one episode of the *Party Down* TV series and the Comedy Central series *Kröd Mändoon and the Flaming Sword of Fire*. Unfortunately, both series were cancelled after the first year.

Hart continued to build a reputation for himself by making cameo appearances in *Death at a Funeral* and *Little Fockers*. He also played the leading role in the comedy film *Something Like a Business*. Most of the reviews were negative, and the film is rarely talked about. But the negative reviews and cancellations didn't

When Hollywood didn't respond as enthusiastically as he'd hoped, Hart decided to go back to performing stand-up on the stages of small clubs. This grounded him and reminded him of what he loved to do.

● ●

bother him. And although he admits that he regrets doing *Something Like a Business*, he still looks at it and his other less successful career moves as opportunities to put his name out there to increase his fan base and to enhance his reputation as a funny, down-to-earth guy.

Turning Pain into Comedy

While he was dealing with the ups and downs of his success, Hart was also dealing with a failing marriage. After being together for almost ten years, Kevin and Torrei Hart separated. Torrei blamed their breakup on Kevin's increasing fame, and she claimed that he had a girlfriend. Although he denied having a girlfriend, Kevin did take some of the blame by saying that he was too young when he got married, and he "didn't really understand the definition of marriage . . . wasn't ready for it."[7]

Following his comedic style, Kevin's separation from Torrei became part of his act in his second stand-up album, *Seriously Funny*. The show premiered on Comedy Central and became one of the fastest selling DVDs in recent years. In front of a sold-out crowd at the Allen Theatre in Cleveland, Ohio, Hart talked about not only his failing marriage and other personal issues but also his fears. But not everyone saw the humor in Hart's skit about his fears.

> "Something can be a joke and true at the same time.[8]"

In *Seriously Funny*, Hart jokes, "one of my biggest fears is my son growing up and being gay. That's a fear. Keep in mind, I'm not homophobic . . . Be happy. Do what you want to do. But me, as a heterosexual male, if I can prevent my son from being gay, I will." Hart later explained that he wasn't trying to upset anyone. As in all of his performances, he gets personal, joking about his life and his fears. "It's about my fear. I'm thinking about what I did as a dad . . . it's me . . . because of my own insecurities."[9] Hart explains that he wouldn't purposely tell a joke to offend people. This same joke brought more attention later in his career when he refused to accept a role as a gay man.

CHAPTER FOUR

Doing Things the Kevin Hart Way

• •

At the young age of thirty-three, Kevin Hart did something that was unheard of in Hollywood: he spent his own money on his own production. He talked with a number of studios about financing his next stand-up comedy tour, Laugh at My Pain, but all of the studios turned him down. So he decided to take a risk and invest $750,000 of his own money to shoot and distribute the film.

It made more than $7 million and is listed as the ninth-highest-grossing stand-up film in history. While using pyrotechnics as a spotlight for his punch lines, Hart jokes about his marriage and separation from Torrei and memories of school events with his dad in his younger years. He even uses humor to deal with the death of his mother and how his family coped with it at the funeral. "I touch on a lot of issues that I chose not to talk about for some time," Hart explains. "As I've grown and matured, I figured out a way to let my audience in on my life as a whole."[1] Hart makes it clear that his jokes are

Kevin Hart's Concert Rider

When performers go on tour, they have to work out a contract with each venue where they perform. The contracts typically include information about security, insurance policies, and fees. The performers also provide a set of requests as a part of the contract. This list of requests is called a concert rider, also known as a tour rider. Items listed on various performers' riders have included anything from food and drinks to candles, lotions, and speakers. In addition to specific dressing room décor, Kevin Hart's tour rider usually includes:

Baked whole wings and seasoned fried wings (forty pieces of each)

Fried chicken tenders (enough for six people)

Cheesesteak wraps (ten)

Assorted cookies (enough for four)

To-go containers (twenty)

Red Bull (sixteen) and assorted Vitaminwaters

Red plastic cups (seventy-five)

Full bar with all beverages chilled, except alcohol

not a blow to his family. "It's never specifically about my family," he explains. "It's about my life within the crazy realm that I grew up in. I'm speaking about my family, but I'm talking about my reaction to what I've seen."[2]

The theatrical version of *Laugh at My Pain*, which Hart codirected, begins with the comedian visiting his hometown of North Philadelphia and stopping by his school, the recreation center where he swam, and his favorite steak sandwich shop, where he leaves money to buy all of the patrons in the shop a sandwich. The scene then changes to his one-hour live performance at L.A. Live's Nokia Theatre. The last ten minutes of the movie show a short film of Hart and the Plastic Cup Boyz reenacting a bank robbery scene from the 1992 crime film *Reservoir Dogs*, which is about a group of criminals and a jewelry heist that goes wrong.

Laugh at My Pain was the first movie produced by Hart's new entertainment company, HartBeat Productions, along with CodeBlack Entertainment, Comedy Central Films, and Usual Suspects Productions. HartBeat Productions is a company of twelve people, including Hart's personal photographer and videographer, Kevin Kwan, who records Hart's every move, partly for social media and partly for his personal archives. Hart wants people to see that just because he is a celebrity, he isn't much different from them. He likes to use social media to show people what a regular day is like for him.

Hart refers to the group of friends that make up HartBeat Productions as the Plastic Cup Boyz. This group includes Harry Ratchford, the director of operations for HartBeat Productions, and Hart's executive assistant, Dwayne Brown. But most people know the Plastic Cup Boyz as the comedy trio—Will "Spank" Horton, Na'im Lynn, and Joey Wells—who

One of the many phrases Hart repeats in his comedy acts—
"Alright! Alright! Alright!"—was a feature on his *Laugh at My Pain*
documentary movie poster. This and other lines from Hart's acts
are such a hit with his fans that they use them on an everyday basis.

opens for Hart on his tours. Kevin and Will have known each other since they were teenagers living in neighboring communities. Na'im, who has been opening for Kevin since 2001, met him while Kevin was hosting a show at Temple University, where Na'im was attending. Joey and Kevin met when Kevin was performing at a club that Joey was hosting.

HartBeat

Hart and his crew were involved in his earlier productions from the start. Through his involvement, Hart learned that he is not only an entertainer but also a businessman. In addition to his ambitions of becoming a comedy idol and an actor, he wanted to be closely involved with the business side of his career. He wanted to own his work and didn't want to work for other people for the rest of his life. He created HartBeat Productions "from scratch from just a vision of what I wanted it to be like . . . I need to be involved."[3] This was a courageous move for Hart because a person who is involved in every part of the entertainment business has to be knowledgeable in all aspects of it. Jeff Clanagan, the CEO of CodeBlack Entertainment, explained that although being so involved in all of the areas of the entertainment business wasn't easy, he had no doubts that Hart could do it because he has no problem being the entertainer and then switching over to "put on the CEO hat. There are not many people who can do the show and the business."[4]

And when Hart says "involved," he doesn't mean just the business end; he also wants to be involved with his fans. And he knows the best way to do this is to connect with

What Does a Production Company Do?

A production company oversees the making of recorded entertainment, such as films, or live entertainment, such as stand-up comedy tours. It also handles the budgets, schedules, scripts, cast, crew, and overall management of the production. The staff of a production company can include actors, directors, film editors, videographers, and photographers. Production companies that produce live shows might also take care of the accommodations for sound and visual needs and hire venue staff. Like Kevin Hart, many comedians and actors are choosing to start their own production companies so that they can be more involved with all parts of the entertainment business. Some comedians who have created their own production companies include Chris Rock, Will Ferrell, Will Smith, and Adam Sandler.

his fans through social media. Hart explains that social media is the best way to prove immediate success and to personally reach his fans. By the end of 2011, he had nearly four million followers on his Facebook fan page, nearly two million followers on Twitter, and a YouTube channel with more than eighty-nine thousand subscribers and more than twenty-two million views. Most of his overseas fans first heard about him on YouTube.

To further connect with his fans, HartBeat Productions along with CodeBlack Interactive developed the Little Jumpman app, "a vertically-challenged game of skill that will make you laugh and cry with Kevin as he reaches for the sky."[5] The app also allows users to connect to Hart's Facebook, Twitter, and YouTube accounts, and at the time of its release, fans were able to use the app to buy tickets in advance for his Laugh at My Pain tour. A few years later, HartBeat Productions created KEVMOJI, an app that includes stickers, emojis, GIFs, and even animated stickers—all depicting photos of Hart and many of his famous catchphrases.

Between Hart's three successful tours and his outreach on social media, it wasn't surprising that he was chosen to host the 2011 Black Entertainment Television (BET) Awards. BET is a television network that targets African American audiences. The annual BET Awards were created to celebrate the achievements of entertainers of color over the previous year. When the network asked fans and entertainers who should host the awards, according to Stephen Hill, BET's president of music programming and specials, "one name came back to us loud and clear: Kevin Hart. He is a blue flame right now."[7] A "blue flame" is a young person who is full of energy and, in business, is willing to do nothing but work.

> "Visual media is huge . . . So I'm just trying to get my hand on it early.[6]"

An Emphasis on Family

Toward the end of 2011, Kevin and Torrei Hart finalized their divorce, and Kevin filed for and received joint custody of their two children. Initially after their separation, there was some animosity between Kevin and Torrei. Torrei publicly accused Kevin of committing infidelity during their marriage, but Kevin denied her claims. Kevin admitted that he made some mistakes and that it was "no way her [Torrei's] fault. I made too many mistakes, we will be better apart."[8]

For years following the divorce, Torrei exchanged words with Kevin's girlfriend, Eniko Parrish, through social media, with Torrei claiming that Eniko was the reason her marriage with Kevin failed, although Eniko denied it. Torrei also expressed that she was uncomfortable with her children living with the woman who broke up their marriage. Eventually, the two women reconciled, and Kevin and Torrei remain close friends—so close, in fact, that Kevin gave Torrei a Cadillac Escalade for her birthday in 2015. Not long after Torrei's birthday, Kevin posted a picture on Instagram of himself with his two children as well as Eniko and Torrei, writing, "As a MAN it's my job to make sure that the two most important women in my life have a relationship. I want to take the time to personally stand up and applaud Eniko and Torrei!"[9]

The most important thing in Kevin Hart's life is his family. Between all of his tours and movies, he enjoys hanging out with his celebrity friends or spending time with his crew at the office. But he spends most of his time off with his kids. He admits that it's not quite a day off because Heaven and Hendrix "run me in a hole. But I love it, love it."[10] Because he is constantly on the move, flying home between film shootings only to leave a few hours later, Hendrix, Heaven, and Eniko will often travel

Keeping his family happy and continuing a close friendship with his ex-wife is one of Hart's highest priorities. When he was honored with a star on the Hollywood Walk of Fame, he invited Torrei (*left*) to join him with his kids and his second wife, Eniko.

with him. He will rent a large house for them while he is on the set filming a movie or on the stage. Hart's kids are often seen with him at celebrity events or onstage helping him accept one of his many awards. Even when he is home but still working, Heaven and Hendrix will hang out at HartBeat's office, which is just around the corner from their house. As a parent, Hart's celebrity status automatically transfers to Hendrix and Heaven, but he wants to make sure that they all keep a balance between celebrity life and real life. As he explains, "I'm a dad first. The business comes second."[11] He keeps them all in touch with reality, helping them with homework, wrestling with them on the couch, or punishing them for cussing; they have a swear jar, so anytime someone cusses, including Hart, a dollar is put into the jar.

> "As a child, there's nobody cooler than your dad. If there is, something's wrong. [12]"

CHAPTER FIVE

Kevin Explains Himself

• • • • • • • • • • • •

B y this point in his career, Hart was doing so well that he was able to finance his third international tour, Let Me Explain, and its film. His ten-month tour included ninety-three shows and generated more than $32 million in ticket sales. Like his other tours, Let Me Explain was turned into a theatrical version, which was released in 2013. The film, produced by HartBeat Productions and CodeBlack Films, features his sold-out performance at Madison Square Garden as well as clips from his performances in other sold-out venues around the world, including Oslo, Amsterdam, Copenhagen, London, and Canada.

The *Let Me Explain* film follows a storyline in which his friends tell him he has changed since his divorce. They won't let him explain himself, so he decides to do a show at Madison Square Garden to explain himself to his audience. Although the film received some negative reviews, with some critics stating that the clips from his tour seemed more like

The Noble Richard Pryor

Richard Pryor, stand-up comedian and actor, is considered the most influential stand-up comedian in history. Comedian Jerry Seinfeld referred to him as "the Picasso of our profession" and, according to Chris Rock, "his very presence gave black people a chance to laugh and feel good about stuff" that would typically make them angry.[1]

Pryor was a no-holds-barred comedian. His performances included harsh views of racism and current issues. Pryor starred in more than forty movies, and he was half of what became Hollywood's first successful interracial comedy act; his other half was comedian Gene Wilder.

Pryor struggled through life, but he appreciated his successes. He described his life best by stating, "I had some great things and I had some bad things, the best and the worst. In other words, I had a life."[2] Richard Pryor passed away in December 2005.

a documentary in which Hart was patting himself on the back, *Let Me Explain* has become the fourth-highest-grossing stand-up comedy film, following *Richard Pryor: Live on the Sunset Strip*, *The Original Kings of Comedy*, and *Eddie Murphy Raw*.

Hoop Dreams

About the same time that the Let Me Explain tour started, Hart was chosen to play for the East team in

Hart was given the opportunity to live one of his childhood dreams— to be an NBA professional player—at the annual NBA All-Star Celebrity Game. Although he can't help but provide entertainment for the crowds, he is a serious hoops player.

• •

the National Basketball Association (NBA) All-Star Celebrity Game. The All-Star Celebrity Game includes former NBA players, actors, musicians, and even government officials. Hart played against a team that included three NBA legends, all at least one foot taller than he is. But using his high school basketball skills and sense of humor, Hart scored eight points, had six assists, and was ejected from the game for attempting to undress on the court. Then he took off his shoes and threw them across the court after receiving two technical fouls, all in good fun.

Although he was thrown out of the game, Hart was voted the Most Valuable Player (MVP). He went on to receive MVP the following three years. After his fourth game, he retired as a celebrity game player but went on to coach the 2016 Team USA against Canada. In the third quarter of the 2016 game, determined "to crush Canada," Hart left his coaching responsibilities at the sidelines and placed himself in the game.[3] Unfortunately, his return didn't make much difference, and Canada won by ten points.

A Knack for Improvisation

Two months after his NBA appearance, the back-to-back release of two movies gave Hart the opportunity to show off his universal skills. *Think Like a Man*—a romantic comedy based on a relationship advice book written by one of the Original Kings of Comedy, Steve Harvey—made more than $30 million in its opening weekend. Hart explains that his leading role as Cedric in the movie was his favorite because "I got to be myself. I got to do what I wanted to do for a long time, which is cut loose and go all out."[4] His second favorite character was Shawn, a burglar, in *Paper Soldiers*.

In many films, especially more dramatic, serious films, the actors have to go by the script. They may be able to improvise somewhat, but not much. One of the aspects of comedy films that Hart likes is how the actors are often allowed to improvise, meaning that they can change the script by adding different lines or by changing some small parts of a scene. In *Think Like a Man*, especially, director Tim Story allowed the actors to bring in some of their own ideas to the film. If their improv didn't work, the actors would go with the original script in that scene.

Think Like a Man also gave Hart the opportunity to move from urban films to mainstream films. His goal as an entertainer is to appeal to more than "just one specific audience. You want to be funny to black people, white people, and Chinese people . . . whoever it is." *Think Like a Man* and his next upcoming movie, *The Five-Year-Engagement*, put Hart in a place where he could

What Are Urban and Mainstream Films?

An urban film is a film genre of independent films that feature mainly African American or Hispanic American culture and typically appeal to that specific population. Often, independent films have a lower budget than mainstream films. This lack of money limits the production company in a number of ways. For instance, the locations where the movie is filmed and the number of theaters it is released in are limited and the actors in independent films are usually unknown.

Mainstream, or commercial, films typically follow a storyline that is most popular with mainstream audiences. Because these films are usually produced by a major film studio, the budget is much higher, which allows the producers to hire A-list actors, to film in expensive and easily recognized locations, to use special effects, and to release the films to a much wider audience than independent films are able to do.

show the mainstream audience that he can be a universal actor and comedian, which is just what he wanted. After the release of *Think Like a Man*, Dave Becky says, "the offers started pouring in."[5]

The Five-Year Engagement, another mainstream romantic comedy, was released only a week after *Think Like a Man*. This film gave Hart a chance to show a different side of himself. Usually seen as the comic relief in his films, he had to curb his energy to fit the somewhat more serious role of his character and of the film's plot.

Hart also played a small role in the film *Exit Strategy*, and he appeared in two episodes of the television series *Modern Family* and in one episode of another television series, *Workaholics*. Both series are still going strong. He also appeared in more than twenty episodes of MTV's *Wild 'n Out*. Between 2007 and 2015, Hart played various roles on the comedy and improv television series, including celebrity guest captain as well as the host of the show when Nick Cannon, the creator of the series, needed someone to fill in for him.

Host with the Most

Hart also appeared on MTV as the host of the 2012 MTV Video Music Awards (VMAs). MTV asked Hart to host "because he has the ability to mix it up with famous people while maintaining the awestruck nature of a . . . fan."[6] One year earlier, he made an appearance at the 2011 VMAs. He delivered an opening monologue and starred in some short skits throughout the show. Although MTV asked him at the last minute, Hart was just as excited to help out in 2011 as he was to host in 2012.

When Hart hosted the 2011 BET Awards, he wrote and performed a short skit called "Househusbands of Hollywood." It was such a hit that he turned it into an award-winning television series, *Real Husbands of Hollywood*, which debuted in January 2013. The series, which is not only written by Hart but also produced by HartBeat Productions along with JSF Productions,

Hart received the NAACP Entertainer of the Year Award, considered the most coveted award of all the Image Awards. In his speech, he said that it was hard to believe that the dream he has been working so hard to achieve is becoming a reality.

received the 2014 and 2015 National Association for the Advancement of Colored People (NAACP) Image Awards for Outstanding Comedy Series.

Hart also won NAACP Outstanding Actor in a Comedy Series in 2014 for his role in *Real Husbands*. The NAACP is an African American civil rights organization located in the United States. It was formed in 1909 "to ensure the political, educational, social, and economic equality of rights of all persons and to eliminate race-based discrimination."[7] The NAACP Image Awards began in 1967 to honor individuals for achievement in the arts and entertainment. When Hart received the 2014 NAACP Image Award, he dedicated it to his mom, saying I'm a "real mama's boy."[8]

> "Everything happens for a reason.[9]"

Hart was also voted the 2016 People's Choice Awards Favorite Cable TV Actor for *Real Husbands*. The People's Choice Awards is an American awards show that was developed in 1975 to recognize individuals and works of popular culture. The awards are based on votes from the general public.

One year after his two back-to-back movies and after his recent awards for his new comedy series, Hart was honored to show off his skills as the host of *Saturday Night Live* (*SNL*). A few years earlier, he had auditioned for SNL but didn't make the cut. At the time, he felt he had no talent. But later he admitted that it was the toughest audition in his life, and it didn't stop him from moving on. Hart even called the comedian whom he was up against in the audition, Dean Edwards, to congratulate him. "If you don't get something, don't let it get you down," Hart explains. "There's something better for you. I'm a prime example . . . dreams come true."[10]

The Importance of Giving Back

Hart loved to show how his dreams came true, and he did it in many different forms. He donated $250,000 to Philadelphia's school districts, parks, and recreation centers to buy new computers. While he visited his hometown to host the Philly 4th of July Jam, he had an opportunity to talk to Philadelphia mayor Michael Nutter. The mayor told Hart how badly the school system was hit after district budget cuts, and Hart decided that he needed to do something about it. He not only made a donation but also announced it in person to the students while visiting some of the district schools and attending a pep rally. Hart tweeted, "I'm personally coming to Philly this FRIDAY to visit & talk to the kids at some of the schools that I will be donating computers to #Philly."[11]

The money he donated supplied the recreation centers with two hundred computers, and three hundred were donated to the Philadelphia school district. Unfortunately, less than one month later, four of the computers were stolen from Cobbs Creek Recreation Center. As soon as Hart heard about the theft, he tweeted to express his anger: "I was just informed that some of the computers that I donated

Kevin Hart uses every opportunity he can to spend time with his kids. Here, his son Hendrix and daughter Heaven join him onstage at the third annual Philly 4th of July Jam.

to the Philadelphia Public School System were stolen," he said. "This is a message to all of the kids at the schools that were affected . . . ignorance like this only motivates me to do more."[12]

Viral Video Star

Hart also loved to promote his work and his success, and he spent a lot of time promoting his films through radio and television interviews and on social media. In 2013, Hart and rapper/actor Ice Cube took a joy ride with talk show host Conan O'Brien in a Lyft car to promote their upcoming movie, *Ride Along*. The video premiered on *Conan* and became one of the top videos on YouTube. In another episode of *Conan* in 2016, the trio took a ride with a student driver to promote the sequel to *Ride Along*. Hart has also been a guest on other talk shows, including nine appearances on the *Ellen DeGeneres Show* and appearances on the *Oprah Winfrey Show*. He also made five appearances on the *Tonight Show Starring Jimmy Fallon*. Hart and Fallon have gone on a few crazy adventures together, like riding a roller coaster at Universal Studios and visiting a haunted house, Blood Manor, supposedly New York City's scariest haunted house. On both adventures, they wore body cameras and were followed by a videographer. Both videos hit the top of the YouTube list.

> "My city made me who I am today and for that I am thankful.[13]"

Hart was honored with the opportunity of a lifetime to show off his acting skills alongside Hollywood legends Sylvester Stallone and Robert De Niro in *Grudge Match*.

• •

In 2013, Hart made a cameo appearance in *This Is the End* and appeared in one episode of the TV series *Second Generation Wayans*. He also played Dante Slate Jr., a fast-talking sports promoter, in the sports comedy *Grudge Match*. He appeared alongside two well-known veteran actors, Sylvester Stallone and Robert De Niro. Hart, honored to be working with the two seasoned veterans, compared his excitement to a kid in a candy store.

And although his year was going well with the release of his *Let Me Explain* album, his new television series, and his many other appearances on both the big and small screens, there was a little bump along with way. In April, Hart was arrested for driving under the influence. He was seen speeding down a freeway, and when he spotted the police following behind him with sirens on, Hart willingly pulled over. He could have easily tried to talk the officers out of arresting him, using his status as a celebrity, but when the officer asked him to take a sobriety test, he told them there was no need and admitted to being drunk. Hart was arrested and held on a $5,000 bond.[14] He later tweeted to his fans, "Drinking & driving is not a game or a laughing matter. This is a wake up call for me, I have to be smarter & last night I wasn't."[15] Soon after this setback, Hart decided he wasn't taking any more chances, so he purchased a fully accessorized Mercedes Sprinter van that he and his family can relax in while being chauffeured around Los Angeles.

CHAPTER SIX

"I Will Sleep When I Die"

K evin Hart was once asked if he was ever going to take a break. His answer: "I don't see the benefit of that [taking time off to relax]. That's how you get left behind."[1] But many seriously wonder when he sleeps, especially when he appears in four movies and three commercials in one year, as he did in 2014. According to his personal videographer Kevin Kwan, Hart, while staying out all night with friends and then driving "right to the plane and playing video games during the entire flight, and then going straight to the next stand-up show,"[2] never complains. Some friends have said that is the reason he is always on the move. Rawson Marshall Thurber, the director of *Central Intelligence*, explains it best when he says, "[Hart is] a master at hiding his fatigue behind a facade of manic enthusiasm. Kevin is like my dad when you put on a movie. If he stops moving, he'll fall asleep."[3]

Ice Cube describes it best by saying, "You cannot not have fun with Kevin Hart."[4] Ice Cube teamed up with

Hart and Ice Cube traveled the globe to promote their movie *Ride Along*. Pairing the quick-witted and self-deprecating comedian with the serious actor-rapper proved to be comedy gold.

Hart to film *Ride Along*, an action comedy released in theaters in January 2014. It was number one for three weeks, and it surpassed ticket sales expectations. It broke the record as the highest-grossing movie to be released during Martin Luther King Jr. weekend and for a movie opening in January. Hart received the Teen Choice Award for Choice Movie Actor: Comedy for his role in *Ride Along*; some even compared him to Eddie Murphy. Responding to this comparison, Hart said it was an honor, but added that Eddie Murphy has "accomplished so much, he's on his own pedestal."[5] Hart wants to create his own legacy rather than be compared to others. These

Who Is O'Shea Jackson Sr.?

O'Shea Jackson Sr. is the actor and rapper known as Ice Cube. He was born on June 15, 1969, in Los Angeles, California. As a rapper, Ice Cube is known for his influential and harsh lyrics. He started his career with hip-hop group C.I.A. and then later joined the rap group N.W.A. He left N.W.A. in 1989 to build a solo career in music and films.

Between 1990 and 2010, Ice Cube produced nine studio albums. He made his film debut as "Doughboy" in the coming-of-age drama *Boyz n the Hood* in 1991, for which he won the Chicago Film Critics Most Promising Actor Award. Since then Ice Cube has appeared in thirty-five movies, nineteen of which he was involved with the production and/or writing. He also made appearances in a number of television series.

comedians are such an influence on him that he has displayed paintings of them throughout his home.

Rethinking the "Black Movie Category" Label

Around the same time that *Ride Along* grossed $100 million, *About Last Night* was released. A remake of a 1986 romantic comedy based on a 1974 play, some say it was better than the original movie. The movie received mixed reviews, but all reviews regarding Hart were good. *San Francisco Chronicle*'s Mick LaSalle describes him as "an excellent comic actor, very funny but always thinking and feeling, staying open and playing off the other actors."[6] Hart was excited to play a leading role in a movie that gave him an opportunity to show a different side of himself. Producer William Packer praises his work, describing it as "a different perspective and point of view than anybody else."[7]

Like many of Hart's other movies, such as *Think Like a Man* and *Ride Along*, *About Last Night* was labeled as a "black movie" because the cast was predominantly African American. These movies were, however, appealing to a mainstream audience, which confirms Hart's view that the label is a stigma that is slowly dying. As Hart explains, "*Ride Along* to even *Think Like a Man* . . . are just good movies . . . movies that everybody's going to see . . . people are going to associate this [*About Last Night*] as being a good movie regardless of the color of the cast."[8] So when a fan accused Hart of doing stereotypical black movies, he tweeted a reply: "I want u 2 realize that people with ur mindset & level of thinking are the reason why our movies get categorized."[9] He went on to defend himself by explaining that he was currently promoting *Ride Along 2* internationally and that he was working hard to remove the "black movie" label from projects that black actors do.

The fact that his stand-up audiences, which were once 60 to 70 percent African American, are now made up of racially diverse crowds shows how hard Hart has worked to change the mind-set that some have about him and other actors of color. He wants people to realize that he has been "approach[ing] it on a universal level. If you associate yourself with one group of people, you alienate another twelve."[10] So he figures out how he can take one thought and make it broader so that it will appeal to everyone.

Although Hart is working hard to get rid of this label, he says that he will "be the first to say there's some films that should be called black movies,"[11] and he admits to having done a few himself earlier in his career, including *Something Like a Business* and *35 and Ticking*. The romantic comedy *35 and Ticking*, in which Hart plays a leading role, had a limited screening release in 2011. The film, which was directed by Russ Parr, who also directed *Something Like a Business*, was supported by the African American Film Critics Association (AAFCA) Seal of Approval program, which seeks "to support talented filmmakers and film marketers by providing them with a direct link to our devoted film followers."[12] According to the AAFCA, *35 and Ticking* "is a part of a national movement of black-themed films released independently in theatres," attracting audiences and flourishing outside of the big studio system."[13] In other words, *35 and Ticking* was one of a number of AfricanAmerican–themed independent films that was more successful than many major film studios expected.

Getting Slimed

One month after *About Last Night* was released, Hart received the Favorite Funny Star Award from the 27th Annual Nickelodeon Kids' Choice Awards. The awards ceremony honors the year's best actors and musicians voted by Nickelodeon viewers. Each year, the ceremony also includes a surprise "sliming" of some of the celebrities and the host of the ceremony. The 2014 host, Mark Wahlberg, the actor in *Transformers: Age of Extinction*, claimed that he would not get slimed, but Hart, being the prankster that he is, wasn't going to let Wahlberg end the show without sliming him. Throughout the show, Wahlberg had a couple of close calls with the slime and continued to brag that he was "unslimeable." But, toward the end of the show, while the audience and other celebrities caused a distraction, Wahlberg's children, with Hart's help, covered him in slime.

By this point in his career, Hart had ten million Instagram followers and more than fourteen million Twitter followers. He likes to promote his work, whether it's his own stand-up shows and productions or other production companies' films, through social media. And he expects to get paid for it. But not everyone agrees with that.

After his next movie, *Think Like a Man Too*, was released, the computers and emails at Sony Pictures, a

Mark Wahlberg's children weren't going to let their dad get out of Nickelodeon's 27th Annual Kids' Choice Awards ceremony without being slimed. Kevin Hart wouldn't allow it either.

distributor of the film, were hacked. The hack involved all divisions of Sony, including Screen Gems, one of the producers of *Think Like a Man Too*. An email from the president of Screen Gems, Clint Culpepper, to Sony heads was published as a result of the hack. In the email Culpepper called Hart unethical because, in addition to the money he was receiving for his part in the movie, he asked for money to promote the movie through social media. Hart responded to the insults in an Instagram stating, "Knowing your self worth is extremely important people . . . I worked very hard to get where I am today. I look at myself as a brand and because of that I will never allow myself to be taken advantage of."[14]

> **"Do you know how much time and energy it takes to hold a grudge?[15] "**

After the incident, Hart explained that he didn't hold any grudges against Culpepper. Although he did react quickly to the leaked email by posting on Instagram, he later admitted that Culpepper called and apologized almost immediately after the comments were released to the public. Hart never intended to confront Culpepper. The two had been friends for years and, according to Hart, that is the way Culpepper talks and the way actors and production studios negotiate. The hard feelings were forgotten, and Hart and Screen Gems worked together in the production of the 2015 film *The Wedding Ringer*.

Never Stop Working

Shortly after *Think Like a Man Too* was released, the comedy-drama *School Dance* was released. Hart made an unbilled, or uncredited, cameo appearance in the film. A few months later, *Top Five*, a movie written and directed by one of his role models and friends, Chris Rock, was released. Rock plays a comedian trying to make it as an actor, and Hart is his fast-talking agent.

Chris Rock: One of the All-Time Great Comedians

Chris Rock started as a stand-up comedian in 1984 in New York City's Catch a Rising Star, which is a chain of comedy clubs. When Eddie Murphy saw Rock performing at a nightclub, he began mentoring Rock and gave him his debut role in *Beverly Hills Cop III*. Rock later became nationally recognized as a member of *Saturday Night Live*. In 1991, Rock released his first comedy album, *Born Suspects*.

Between 1985 and 2016, Rock has appeared in more than forty films, and between 1997 and 2003, he won four Emmy Awards and three Grammy Awards. He was also voted the fifth-greatest stand-up comedian in a poll conducted by Comedy Central. The work of Rock, who has worked as a comedian, actor, writer, producer, and singer, has focused on his teenage experiences and involves class and race relations, politics, and family.

Along with his successful year in the movies, Hart teamed up with a few companies to show off his comedic talent in commercials. He promotes Fandango gift cards in its "One Size Fits All" commercial by poking fun at his small stature. In Glacéau Vitaminwater's "Make It Big" commercial, Hart makes fun of his career as a shoe salesman and his early career as a stand-up comedian. Appearing during the 2014 NBA play-offs, the main message of the "Make It Big" commercial was to work hard to get what you want.

He also teamed up with actor Dave Franco and EA Sports to promote the 2015 *Madden NFL* video game. Hart adds a new talent in this promotion. The commercial includes not only his comedic and acting talent but also a rap video with lyrics sung by Hart. He ended his successful year as the recipient of the *People Magazine* Comedy Star of the Year Award.

Thanking His Fans

His next appearance was a leading role in *The Wedding Ringer*, which was released at the beginning of 2015. Hart played Jimmy Callahan, the owner and CEO of Best Man, Inc., who provides grooms-to-be with best men. Although the movie received many negative reviews, it was a box office hit and generated more than $79 million. Some of that money came from Hart when he bought out a movie theater for two showings and announced through Instagram that he was giving away five hundred tickets to his fans in Toledo, Ohio, for his recently released movie. He later tweeted, "since my comedy shows sold out so fast I felt that it was only right

Kevin Hart is known for his philanthropic contributions. Like anyone, however, he enjoys spending some of his hard-earned money on presents for himself, like his "Bat mobile"—a Mercedes Benz SLS AMG.

to treat the rest of my fans."[16] He also tweeted that he was giving away one hundred tickets to Charlotte, North Carolina, fans to see his *Laugh at My Pain* film. When he showed up at the AMC Carolina Pavilion theater, Hart decided to give away two hundred tickets instead.

This is just an example of the ways he has shared his wealth with his fans. Although he is known to reward himself with the money he receives from his stand-up tours and various movie roles—Hart bought a Ferrari 458 Spider from his *Let Me Explain* earnings, a 1966 Pontiac GTO from *The Wedding Ringer*, and his house from *Think Like a Man*—he also likes to put his money toward useful causes. In April 2015, he joined with the

United Negro College Fund and donated $50,000 to each of four Philadelphia high school seniors. Hart chose the recipients "based on their grade point average and their need of financial assistance in order to pursue higher education."[17] He recognized his contribution as his way of "stepping up to the plate and saying what you're doing is dope,"[18] meaning "excellent."

Hart also contributes to other charitable organizations such as the Alzheimer's Association, the GOOD+ Foundation, and the NAACP. In 2013, Hart hosted HartBeat Weekend with the intention to show off his favorite talents in comedy and music. This annual event has since become an event to give back to the community as well. In the first three annual events, Hart worked with Gifts of Hope, Syracuse University Project Advance, and Britticares International.

> "It's vital to give back. It's something we can all do.[19]"

Bad Timing

In his next feature role, Hart costarred with comedian Will Ferrell in *Get Hard* in 2015. Hart played blue-collar car washer Darnell Lewis, and Ferrell played James King, a white-collar worker heading for prison. James assumes that, because Darnell is black and washing cars for a living, he has been in prison before, and James offers to hire Darnell to help him toughen up for prison life. Although Darnell had never been to prison, he takes advantage of James and his offer. The movie received many negative reviews but not because of the acting. The timing of the film's release was bad luck, and the movie was seen as racist and offensive.

Less than one year before *Get Hard* was released, an unarmed black teenager was shot and killed by a white police officer in Ferguson, Missouri. A grand jury decision not to charge the police officer for the murder of an unarmed civilian led to protests for weeks after the incident, both in the St. Louis suburbs and throughout the country. Although many of the demonstrations were peaceful, those in Missouri and in other cities across the country led to buildings being vandalized and cars being flipped and burned, among other

Hart costarred with Will Ferrell in the 2015 box office success *Get Hard.* Even though the two comedians received good reviews, the film was critically panned. Many saw it as offensive because of perceived race-related stereotypes.

acts of violence. In other areas of the country, demonstrators chanting "black lives matter" marched down major highways, putting traffic at a standstill.

When *Get Hard* premiered at the South by Southwest Film Festival (SXSW), an audience member called out to the film's director, Etan Cohen, that the movie's story on black and white assumptions was racist. Cohen explained that when you are doing a comedy, people might get confused about what you're actually making fun of. He also explained that testing was done with mixed audiences to view how different groups reacted. And throughout the making of the movie, he received the opinions of the actors as to whether something might be perceived as too offensive. Will Ferrell emphasized that all R-rated comedies offend someone at some point. Kevin Hart explained that there was actually a lesson to learn in the movie. Two people meet and automatically have opinions of one another because of who they are and what they look like, but "after peeling off some of the layers to their onion, they realize that, 'Oh my God, this isn't the person I thought it was . . . It's a completely different person.' And that road to friendship ensues."[20] But when it comes to addressing his views on racism and racist violence in his stand-up routines, Hart will never do it. He explains, "It's not my style . . . It angers me, but not onstage. Onstage, my job is to take away whatever problems are in the world, for that brief moment of time."[21] The race-themed jokes in the movie, Hart explains, "shows the value of understanding."[22]

CHAPTER SEVEN

Ready, Run, Action

·····································

L ess than a month after the release of *Get Hard*, Hart started his fourth and biggest stand-up comedy tour, What Now? His first appearance was in San Antonio, Texas. He visited forty-five cities and ended his tour in Philadelphia, Pennsylvania, where he performed in front of a sold-out crowd at the Lincoln Financial Field—fifty-three thousand seats. This final show made history, as he was the first comedian to sell out a National Football League (NFL) stadium.

What Now?

At this point in his career, Kevin Hart was known as one of the best comedians in history, and the prices his fans were willing to pay for his What Now? tickets proved it. Fans were paying higher prices for the What Now? show than they would for NFL event tickets. Hart's Philadelphia fans were paying more on average than they would pay to attend two Philadelphia Eagles home games, according to the Eagles' 2015 schedule. At this

Hart gets the crowd laughing at the HartBeat Weekend in Las Vegas, Nevada. The first night featured two stand-up comedy performances of Kevin Hart & Friends Comedy All-Stars, and the second night featured an advanced viewing of *What Now?*

• • • • • • • • • • • • • • • • • • • •

point in his tour, Kevin's hometown fans were paying on average more than $210 for one ticket.

And it wasn't just for his national and international tours that people were willing to pay such high prices to attend. Shortly before his tour officially started, Hart performed a one-hour show at Florida Gulf Coast University. University students paid $35 to see his show; non-university students paid $65. But so many people wanted to attend the show that tickets started appearing online for prices between $200 and $300. Many fans agreed that seeing the show was worth the money.

In total, the What Now? tour sold more than six hundred thousand tickets and grossed more than

No Cell Phones Please!

Kevin Hart's one big rule for all of his live performances: no cell phones. Fans will notice signs posted stating, "FOR KEVIN HART SHOW, NO: Cellphones, texting, tweeting, talking, cameras, recording devices of any kind DURING THE SHOW OR YOU WILL BE EJECTED." It's unknown why Hart is so strict about this. He may want to ensure his fans enjoy the show rather than text and take selfies, or it may be the fact that the show could later be used in films.

Whatever the reason, he means business. One of his concert rider requests includes "roamers," or people employed to walk through the crowds looking for anyone using cell phones. For larger venues, Hart will typically ask for close to one hundred people to roam throughout the venue, twenty people on a team, to remove anyone using a phone and another eight supervisors with radios.

$35 million. Hart planned to donate money from the Philadelphia show to "renovate parks in the inner city, put them in my mother's name, out of my pocket. I'm doing playgrounds because I want something visual that I can be associated with."[1]

Hart's performance at the Lincoln Financial Field was turned into a film that was produced by HartBeat Productions and released in October 2016 at more than 2,500 locations in North America. It became the fifth-highest-grossing stand-up film in history. Hart explains that the *What Now?* movie is "not a concert film—it's an action movie."[2] The film begins with a short skit in which the comedian plays a British secret service agent who then leads Hart to the Lincoln Financial Field. Although he does emphasize his small size by sitting on an unusually large toilet seat when he talks about his fear of public restrooms, he doesn't spend as much time poking fun at himself and his life on this tour as he did on his past tours. Instead, he talks about current events, parenting, and his thoughts on everyday life.

> "I want to be known as a real human being.[3]"

The performance at the Lincoln Financial Field was the last on his national tour, but he wasn't done yet. After a few months off, he went back on the road with his What Now? international tour, which began in January 2016 in Manchester, England. At the end of the full tour, Hart had performed 156 shows and visited 112 cities, 13 countries, and 5 continents.

Spontaneous Runs

The day before Hart sold out the Lincoln Financial Field, he took a run in his hometown of Philadelphia with almost 6,500 people. They ran the streets and mimicked Rocky Balboa from the movie *Rocky* by running up the

Hart is serious about promoting health and fitness. In August 2015, he called out to his fans to join him for a spontaneous run through the streets of Philadelphia. Close to 6,500 people of all ages heard his call and joined him for some fitness fun.

• • • • • • • • • • • • • • • • • • • •

steps of the Philadelphia Museum of Art. This was just one of many of Hart's spontaneous runs.

His first unplanned run took place in Boston, Massachusetts. During his What Now? tour, he decided to fly to Boston after his shows in Baltimore, Maryland, to take a run. He didn't want to run alone so he tweeted his fans, "Breaking News people . . . I'm flying back to Boston tonight after my shows in Baltimore. I'm going to run a spontaneous 5K in the morning."[4] The next morning, about three hundred fans—not all of them runners or even people who enjoy fitness—joined Hart for an early morning run.

Hart ran in thirteen cities within five months, which is amazing for a man who had only recently begun running. He has since become all about fitness. A morning workout is scheduled into his daily routine, he has a personal trainer, Ron "Boss" Everline, and he does one thousand sit-ups each day, but not necessarily all at once, as Hart explains. "I could just lift my knees up like so while we're talking. That's thirty, then I'll go another place and fit in a quick twenty-five."[5]

These spontaneous runs are his way to get people moving for fitness and health wellness. A few months before the Boston run, Hart partnered with Rally Health to serve as its first health ambassador. Rally Health, the sponsor of the What Now? tour, is a digital leader in helping people participate in their own health care in various ways such as education and fitness. Rally Health's Ambassador Program "aims to educate and inspire people to make better, more informed decisions about their health,"[7] and Rally chose Hart because "his passion for fitness and laughter makes him a natural advocate to inspire people to adopt healthier habits."[8]

"If it doesn't hurt, you're not doing it right.[6]"

He also played host at Rally Healthfests, the first taking place in Dallas, Texas. These healthfests are free community events that feature activities such as Zumba lessons, yoga, rock climbing, and cycling classes. They also feature activities for kids, music, and, of course,

Kevin Hart. Throughout the day, Hart will jump around and cheer everyone on. His main goal for the healthfests and the spontaneous runs is to help his fans take that first step in leading healthier lives. He hosted two more Rally Healthfests in 2016 in New York City and Los Angeles, California, and he and Rally Health plan to host many more.

Hart's work with Rally Health and his belief that the "power of sport and maintaining a healthy lifestyle makes you better"[9] caught the attention of Nike. Hart and Nike Run Club teamed up to make his impromptu runs more organized. Nike told him that they loved what he was doing because he was "bridging that gap between professional athlete and the person that doesn't consider themselves an athlete."[10] And they, along with Rally Health, have continued the not-quite-spontaneous runs through his international What Now? tour. In 2015, the running program Run with Hart not only brought together approximately fifteen thousand fans to run with the comedian, but also led to other programs—Move with Hart, which includes boot camp–style workouts and a fitness podcast, and Train with Hart. They all work on the same philosophy of getting everyday people, both those who are into fitness and those who are just beginning, to get out and get fit through running, working out, and training.

Chocolate Droppa and David Beckham

Hart spent a lot of time promoting his What Now? tour with his running and training events as well as through the use of social media. But he didn't stop there. He decided to bring out his rapper persona, Chocolate Droppa, to promote his What Now? tour. In 2011, when Hart hosted the BET Awards, he performed a skit of his alter ego, Chocolate Droppa. Since then, Chocolate Droppa rapped on *Saturday Night Live* in 2015, and he made an appearance on the radio station Real 92.3 LA. In August 2016, Chocolate Droppa signed with Motown Records for his first album, which is a *What Now?* mixtape with seventeen tracks that feature some well-known artists, including singer and songwriter Chris Brown and rapper Big Sean. The album was released around the same time as Hart's What Now? tour's stand-up album.

While Hart was running and touring, he was also working on a commercial with David Beckham. Beckham, an internationally known soccer player, was a major promoter of H&M clothing. Hart and Beckham teamed up to promote its Modern Essentials clothing line. The commercial features Hart playing a method actor who follows Beckham throughout his day and mimics him because Hart wants to know everything about the man he hopes to portray in the soccer star's upcoming (fictional) biography. As he does in his stand-up comedies, Hart uses his personal life, in this case his size, to advertise H&M clothing, specifically noting the fact that Modern Essentials clothing will fit any size, as Beckham is six inches taller than he is. The commercial, which was almost seven minutes long, received great reviews, and a sequel was released in 2016.

Comedic Rockstar

Hart's hard work in 2015 was recognized with the Comedic Genius Award by MTV for his roles in comedy films and television shows such as *Real Husbands of Hollywood* and *Comedy Central Roast of Justin Bieber* for which Hart played host. MTV stated that he deserved the award for "bold and irreverent comedic style that has captivated audiences from his movies and sitcoms, to stand-up specials, award show performances and in front of packed arenas of fans."[11] This was only the second year the award was presented; Will Ferrell, Hart's costar in *Get Hard*, received the award in 2014.

Hart, who normally doesn't take part in comedy roasts, said yes when he was asked to be the roast master at the *Comedy Central Roast of Justin Bieber*. Hart said he had to do it for the twenty-first birthay of "the Biebs."

Hart also appeared on the cover of the July 2015 issue of *Rolling Stone* magazine. When the magazine appeared on the newsstands, Hart shared his excitement with his fans on Instagram, stating that he could "officially check a major goal off of my list . . . That goal was to one day grace the cover of *Rolling Stone* Magazine . . . make sure you read it . . . The title of 'Comedic Rockstar' is now OFFICIAL!!!!!"[12] Between 2012 and 2016, Hart has appeared on more than twenty-five magazine covers, including *Men's Health*, *Men's Fitness*, and *Vibe*.

He then received the official title as the second-highest-paid comedian in 2015 according to *Forbes* magazine rankings. *Forbes* uses data from Box Office Mojo, the Internet Movie Database (IMDb) and interviews with agents and managers, among others, to create its rankings. Between his movie and TV appearances and the What Now? tour, Hart earned $28.5 million. In 2016, he made it to the top of the list, earning $87.5 million, and he was the first comedian to ever earn more than comedian Jerry Seinfeld. His earnings also put him in sixth place as one of the highest-paid celebrities in the world, which includes musicians, athletes, and actors. The ten highest-paid comedians in the world make a combined $233.5 million before taxes and management fees.

CHAPTER EIGHT

All Grown Up Now

I n 2016, Kevin Hart played more than one hundred shows around the world and appeared on both big and small screens. At the beginning of 2016, he received the People's Choice Awards for Favorite Comedic Movie Actor and Favorite TV Cable Actor. Hart also received a Shorty Award for the Best Comedian at the eighth Annual Shorty Awards. With 43.4 million Instagram followers, 30.9 million Twitter followers, more than 23 million Facebook followers, and his own YouTube channel, it's no wonder he was honored as the best comedian behind the most creative work on Facebook, Twitter, YouTube, and Instagram.

And during the Super Bowl, while the Denver Broncos were defeating the Carolina Panthers, Hart's "First Date" Hyundai commercial was earning second place as one of the top performing commercials. The commercial, in which the comedian plays a dad who follows his daughter on her first date and even goes so

What Are the Shorty Awards?

The Shorty Awards were created in 2008 by the technology start-up company Sawhorse Media and were the first awards created "to honor social media. The Shortys remains the most prominent award show of its kind."[1] The first Shorty Awards ceremony was held in 2009 at the Galapagos Art Space, in Brooklyn, NY. Since then, the ceremonies have moved to the New York Times Center and have grown to include celebrity presenters. The voting platform has grown to more than 2.4 million tweeted nominations. Winners are chosen by votes from the public, and scores are given by the Real Time Academy of Short Form Arts & Sciences. The Real Time Academy recognizes social media's top content creators, influencers, and organizations and is responsible for creating the rules of the Shorty Awards and for selecting the winners and honorees.

far as to hitch a ride on a helicopter, received more than two million online views.

Kevin Hart Day

Hart also started off the year with the release of *Ride Along 2*, in which he teams up with Ice Cube once again. Unfortunately, the sequel didn't do nearly as well as the first movie. It received many negative reviews, stating that the film was nearly identical to the first *Ride Along*.

Shortly after the release of *Ride Along 2*, during Black History Month, Hart received an honor no celebrity would take for granted: he was given his own day, Kevin Hart Day. After meeting with many of the senators and other members of the California government on February 22, he was presented with a plaque to commend him for his "professional accomplishments, civic engagement, and commitment to social justice."[2] Senator Isadore Hall explained to the California State Senate that Hart is able to use laughter to help cope with life struggles and to stay out of trouble, and he stated that he is one of the hardest-working people in Hollywood.

Afterward, in Hart's media style, he tweeted "Happy Kevin Hart Day" to his fans. He also asked how people

Both Hart and Dwayne "the Rock" Johnson responded to *Central Intelligence*'s antibullying message. They used promotional opportunities to spread their message against bullying and to show their fans that anyone can be bullied, no matter their size.

thought Kevin Hart Day should be honored. He then came up with his own idea, tweeting, "You can only wear jean shorts on #KevinHartDay. Your knees have to be out on #KevinHartDay."[3]

An Antibullying Message

Around the same time *Ride Along 2* was released, Hart finished shooting *Central Intelligence*. The roles in this movie are reversed a bit for the actors because Hart, typically the comedian, played the serious role, and his costar, Dwayne "the Rock" Johnson, typically the serious action star, played the comedian. The storyline is about two high school classmates who reconnect via Facebook, and while the movie is full of action and comedy, it sends a message about bullying. "Especially now with social media and cyberbullying, it's really an important message to shine a light on that and say this is not OK," explained director Rawson Marshall Thurber. "Even a mean Instagram post can really have an effect."[4]

Hart and Johnson wanted to go farther with their antibullying message and used every opportunity they could, even during their many interviews about *Central Intelligence*. Shortly after the movie's release, they made an unexpected visit to Landmark High School in New York City. According to Johnson, the students at the school face many challenges daily, challenges that both he and Hart know all about. They told the students to overcome their challenges, and "if you are a person who has been bullied . . . speak up. Tell people what is going on."[5]

Hart and Johnson played a part in what was possibly one of the most fun ways to send an antibullying message—for them as well for as their fans—when they partnered with Omaze and the Kind Campaign for a bullying awareness fund-raiser. The Kind Campaign is a nonprofit organization that brings awareness to girl-against-girl bullying and provides information and help about bullying at an international level. Omaze uses technology to help raise awareness and to raise money for charities around the world. When people made donations, their names were entered into a drawing. The two lucky winners were flown to New York to ride in a monster truck with Johnson and Hart through a custom obstacle course with the goal of crushing everything in their path.

Shortly before *Central Intelligence* premiered, Hart suffered what some might say was a form of bullying: his home was burglarized. About $500,000 worth of clothing, jewelry, watches, and other items were taken during the burglary. Fortunately, no one was home at the time, and according to him that was all that mattered. "It's material things. All that stuff can be replaced."[6] A few days after the robbery, Hart posted a photo on Instagram claiming to be of the man who robbed his house. He said his home security cameras captured a picture of the thief. He later admitted that it was actually a stock photo of a man in a ski mask and was only meant to be funny, but he also looked at it as sending a message to the robber. "They've seen the power of social media," explains Hart. "It circulates, gets people talking."[7]

Playing a White Bunny

His third film of that year, *The Secret Life of Pets*, introduced him to the world of animation. In the movie, Hart does the voice for the bad rabbit, Snowball. When he was asked to list one thing he enjoyed most about doing voice-over in an animation movie, he replied, "you can wear your pajamas and it's just you in the booth. I also like doing things my kids can relate to. I curse a lot so my kids can't usually see my movies!"[8] Both fans and movie reviewers gave *The Secret Life of Pets* a thumbs-up. It grossed more than $800 million worldwide, becoming the highest-grossing original animated film not produced by Disney or Pixar. It was so well received that *The Secret Life of Pets 2* is already in the works. Many people feel *The Secret Life of Pets* should be nominated for an Oscar, an award Hart hoped to be honored with earlier in his career.

> "Dog person. One hundred percent . . . Cats are evil.[9]"

Since then, however, Hart has stated that his career isn't about the awards. It is about the support from his fans. But when it comes to *The Secret Life of Pets*, he hopes it will win him an Oscar if for nothing else than the controversy that has been surrounding the Oscars over the past few years. Tagged as the "Oscars So White" campaign, tension had been growing in Hollywood regarding the lack of racial diversity at the Oscars in 2015 and 2016. The controversy first began in 2015 when, for the first time since 1995,

Hart got serious as a presenter at the 88th Annual Academy Awards show, when he addressed the tensions in Hollywood from the "Oscars So White" campaign.

no performers of color were included in the actor nominations. Rather than making changes for the following year, the 2016 Oscars again didn't include any actors of color in the nominations.

Although many actors boycotted the 2016 Oscars, Hart hosted the awards ceremony. And he used this opportunity to discuss the racial tension, stating that "there have been difficult times in Hollywood this year with the Oscars So White controversy overshadowing the ceremony. Accusations of racism and lack of diversity have been propelled to the forefront of the industry."[10]

Hart doesn't think that bringing more attention to the issues is going to make a difference. He wants to "break down some doors so he can be an example of how it can be different."[11] And a black man playing a white bunny is just what he had in mind to help tackle racism in Hollywood. As Hart stated, "You wanna go Oscars So White? I'll give you white. Here's a white bunny."[12]

Training Clothes

At the same time that *The Secret Life of Pets* was released, Nike released the Nike Free Train Instinct Hart training shoe. The sneaker, created with Hart's personal and public inspiration to get fit, has twenty-three of his choice motivational phrases. And according to Hart, they are words that he has "told myself to put that drive back in me. They've gotten me to the place where I am, who knows what it can do for others."[13] Hart promoted the shoe earlier that year on the *The Tonight Show Starring Jimmy Fallon*, when he wore the red version of the shoe, which he dedicated to his daughter. In another appearance on the show, he wore the blue shoes, which are dedicated to his son.

Hart was also busy promoting Foot Locker clothing with Draymond Green. In a commercial, he works with a young actor who is portraying his son, Hendrix, to promote Kids Foot Locker clothing. Once again, the comedian's small stature becomes the joke. His "son" accuses Hart of wearing his clothing, and Hart tries to convince his son that he couldn't fit into his clothes. Hart explains to his son that he isn't small; he is petite. "Petite is just the cooler version of small."[14]

An Online Comedy Network

In July, Hart took advantage of the 2016 Montreal Just for Laughs Comedy Festival to promote his Laugh Out Loud comedy network. At the 2015 Just for Laughs Festival, he decided he wanted to help other creative people achieve success. So his HartBeat Productions partnered with Lionsgate Entertainment company to develop the Laugh Out Loud network. The network, which will launch in 2017, is an online-only service that will include scripted and unscripted series as well as fresh comedians and social media starts. During the 2016 festival, he presented Kevin Hart's Laugh Out Loud Network Pitch Panel to give beginners in the entertainment field a chance to pitch their best pilot ideas for a spot on the network. At the pitch panel, ten finalists were given two minutes to pitch their idea to Hart and his team. He was so impressed by all ten finalists that he agreed to take them all.

Less than fifteen years after his first lead movie role in *Paper Soldiers*, Hart was honored with a star on the Hollywood Walk of Fame. The stars are public monuments recognizing the achievements of individuals in the entertainment industry.

So many seasoned veterans reached out to Hart when he was a fresh comedian, and he hopes the Laugh Out Loud network will give him the chance to do the same for up-and-coming comedians. His first piece of advice to people who want to get into comedy is to go "do it. You can't do things that you don't put actions behind. So sit down, take a piece of paper, write out your thoughts and then go to an amateur night and try them. If it doesn't go well, see what worked, what didn't work and go back and try it again. But don't be a talker, be a doer."[15] To succeed in the entertainment business, Hart says people need to brand themselves. It isn't just about the humor; it's about developing an individual style, meeting people, and, most important, showing respect. People will

91

remember these qualities, bringing them back time and time again.

He was also a part of the all-star panel of judges at the *Jeff Ross Presents Roast Battle* held at the L'Astral Theatre during the Just for Laughs festival. A comedy roast is an event in which a "specific individual is subjected to good-natured jokes at their expense intended to amuse the event's wider audience."[16] Sixteen comedians competed onstage using their best jokes to "burn" their opponent. The judges, including Hart, Whoopi Goldberg, Judd Apatow, among others, determined the best comedian in each dual.

> "You can find a positive in every negative.[17]"

A New Beginning

And if he wasn't busy enough in 2016, Hart married his longtime girlfriend, Eniko Parrish. They had been engaged for two years. The wedding ceremony was held in Santa Barbara, California, on August 13. Both his daughter and son took part in the ceremony. Hart chose his then eight-year-old son, Hendrix, as his best man because, as he explains, "My son is my best friend."[18] Hart explained that he is the great dad that he is because he doesn't want to make the same mistakes his dad made when he was young. He believes that everything happens for a reason, and in his case, he feels that if his dad hadn't made the mistakes he made when he was young, his life might have turned out differently. His dad even admits that, given his

Treating Himself

Although Kevin Hart didn't wear sneakers on his wedding day, he is serious about always wearing sneakers. And he has approximately five hundred pairs to prove it. He even has sneakers that can be worn with tuxedos. When he was young, he always wanted some nice sneakers. His mom didn't have the money to spend on frivolous items like that, so he promised himself that he would one day make enough money to collect sneakers. Hart also has a collection of cars, including a Mercedes Benz SUV and a Mercedes Benz with gull-wing doors. And he loves watches. At last count, Hart owned a dozen Rolexes, five Richard Milles, and a few Patek Philippes and Audemars Piguets. Like his cars, he purchases watches for himself as a reward. And he only buys the ones that will not lose their value. He considers them an investment.

history, it's a miracle that Hart never had a problem with drugs. He was Hart's "example to never go down that road."[19]

Hart credits his dad for helping him to build his character, making him strong, and teaching him how to take care of himself. Even after dealing with his dad's problems, Hart explained that he wouldn't change his life at all. He also credits his dad for the many lines that his fans now recognize and repeat on a daily basis, such as "Alright, alright, alright!" and "You gon' learn today"—phrases he often uses in his comedy acts.

Many years earlier, Kevin's brother, Robert, who is now working to become one of the few black professional billiards players, planned a family intervention for their dad. The intervention led Kevin and Robert to place their dad into a rehabilitation center, where he met a woman who changed his life. When their dad left rehab, Kevin and Robert purchased a house for him, and Kevin and his dad now have a good relationship. Kevin respects his dad for cleaning himself up and not complaining about his past life.

One month after his wedding and honeymoon, Hart began traveling again for his *Hart of the City* series that premiered on Comedy Central in October. The eight-episode series included stops in Atlanta, Houston, Chicago, Sacramento, Miami, Washington, DC, Philadelphia, and Birmingham. In each city, he went to the most well-known local stand-up scenes looking for fresh comedians to feature in *Hart of the City*. Each episode included Hart and the featured comedians talking about the comedy climate in their cities. The premiere of *Hart of the City* followed airings of *Seriously Funny*, *I'm a Grown Little Man*, and *Laugh at My Pain* as part of Comedy Central's Hart-to-Hart-to-Hart Weekend.

Just a few days before the release of his *What Now?* stand-up album in October, Hart was honored with the 2,591st star on the Hollywood Walk of Fame. Ironically, his star is located next to DSW Shoes. His family and many friends, including Ice Cube and Dave Becky, were present at the ceremony when he thanked his family, including his mom, who he said would be so proud of him, and his fans. Hart told his fans, "I don't get here without you and without your support. I am a representation of what you have made me." He then joked, "Please, please don't pee on my star for at least a month. Give me one month."[20]

CHAPTER NINE

What's Next?

E veryone pretty much knows that Kevin Hart doesn't know how to say no. As Snoop Dogg joked at the *Comedy Central Roast of Justin Bieber*, "When it comes to your movie career you never say the N-word, and that's 'no.'" (At that same roast, Snoop Dogg also referred to Hart as "mini-me.")[1] Hart has a career philosophy: "If you stop, or even if you slow down, you're going to look up and realize that somebody has passed you . . . When you get hot, you can choose to stay hot."[2] So it's not surprising to hear that he returned to the big screen in 2017 for three more movies, with a fourth film in the works to be released in 2018.

Hart returned to animation as the voice of George Beard in the action comedy *Captain Underpants*, based on a children's novel series, released in June 2017. He once again costarred with Dwayne Johnson in a sequel of the 1995 film *Jumanji*. The new *Jumanji* is a tribute to the late Robin Williams, a well-known and respected

History of Stand-Up Comedy

Stand-up comedy originated in the Unites States in the nineteenth century with humorists like Mark Twain, who traveled the country telling amusing anecdotes. By the end of the nineteenth century, stand-up comedy turned more toward comedic routines similar to today's comedy skits. Stand-up comedy then became a popular part of American entertainment in the 1930s with the help of Bob Hope, who changed comedy from cliché monologues to jokes about everyday life, news, and current events. This style of comedy could make the audience laugh and at the same time engage them with interesting and current topics. In the late 1960s, stand-up comedians such as George Carlin and Richard Pryor developed a more powerful socially aware and influential style. Today, stand-up comedy continues to be "American culture's primary means of processing and commenting on political leaders, Hollywood gossip, and the headline news of the day."[3]

American stand-up comedian, who passed away in 2014. And finally, Hart played a lead role in a US remake of *The Intouchables*, a 2011 French comedy film. (Some are calling the film *The Untouchables*, "untouchable" being the English word for the French "intouchable.") And there is talk of Hart and Ice Cube teaming up once again for yet another sequel to *Ride Along*.

Hart has admitted that sometimes his success feels surreal to him, but his accomplishments show him that his hard work is paying off. The secret to his success? Work hard and don't quit or give up when something doesn't go your way.

In addition to the release of three more movies, Hart signed a deal with an imprint of the Atria Publishing Group, 37 INK, to publish his memoir, *From the Hart*. He will use the written word rather than the stage to talk about growing up in Philadelphia, dealing with a dad with a drug addiction, and facing the challenges of a young comedian just starting out. And considering that in Hart's almost four decades alive he has accomplished more than most people would in their lifetimes, his memoir should have a lot to say.

Kevin Hart has moved from a one-bedroom apartment in a rough neighborhood

> **"You want to always challenge yourself and show growth as an actor.**[4]**"**

of Philadelphia to a mansion in a gated community in the Los Angeles suburbs. In seventeen years, he has appeared, or will appear, in seventy movies and television shows, not to mention that he wrote, directed, and/or produced more than ten of those films and episodes. He has built a production company from the ground up with a small crew of twelve and has received or been nominated for close to thirty awards.

As a fitness ambassador, he has inspired tens of thousands of people to get fit. And as a comedian, he has broken the records of past comedians—records that were never before broken—and he has

Highly Accomplished

Hart has accomplished so much in less than two decades that it's difficult to keep track of just his movie and television appearances, let alone the many other things he has done. Between 2001 and 2018, according to the IMDb, he has been given seventy credits for his appearances as an actor in movies and TV series, which includes *Captain Underpants, Jumanji, The Intouchables, and Ride Along 3*.[5] (Credits indicate the roles or positions, such as actor, writer, or producer, that an individual plays in productions.) He has thirteen producer credits, thirteen writer credits, and four soundtrack credits. He has appeared in ten commercials, seven of them as the main character, and between 2002 and 2016, he made appearances as himself on more than 140 television series and talk shows. He also received fourteen awards and was nominated for fifteen others between 2004 and 2016.

broken rules of the entertainment business, such as self-funding projects, and is working to break down barriers for entertainers.

Throughout his star-studded career, he has talked about and poked fun at the many people who have inspired or influenced him. Even now as one of the most famous, not to mention richest, comedians in world history, he will admit that he couldn't have done it without the many people who influenced his life and his career. He credits his mom, as well as his dad, for the man he is today. He credits his mentors, such as Keith Robinson and Dave Becky, for helping him achieve his dreams. And he credits many comedians, from Eddie Murphy to Chris Rock to all of the Original Kings of Comedy, for their influence.

Shortly after he finished his What Now? tour, Hart announced that he didn't know if he would ever go on tour again. But only a year before that, he said he would never stop going onstage. He has surprised people from his first night onstage. He may go back to touring or he may stick with films, both acting and producing. But, as he says, "At this point, I'm competing against Kevin Hart."[6]

Films

2001 *North Hollywood* (TV movie)
2002 *Paper Soldiers*
2002 *Class of '06*
2003 *Scary Movie 3*
2004 *Along Came Polly*
2004 *Soul Plane*
2005 *The 40-Year-Old Virgin*
2005 *In the Mix*
2006 *Scary Movie 4*
2006 *The Last Stand*
2007 *Epic Movie*
2007 *The Weekend* (TV movie)
2008 *Fool's Gold*
2008 *Drillbit Taylor*
2008 *Superhero Movie*
2008 *Meet Dave*
2008 *Extreme Movie*
2009 *Not Easily Broken*
2010 *Something Like a Business*
2010 *Death at a Funeral*
2010 *Little Fockers*
2010 *Little in Common* (TV movie)
2011 *35 and Ticking*
2011 *Let Go*

2012 *Think Like a Man*
2012 *Exit Strategy*
2012 *The Five-Year Engagement*
2013 *This Is the End*
2013 *Grudge Match*
2014 *Ride Along*
2014 *About Last Night*
2014 *Think Like a Man Too*
2014 *Top Five*
2015 *The Wedding Ringer*
2015 *Get Hard*
2016 *Ride Along 2*
2016 *Central Intelligence*
2016 *The Secret Life of Pets*
2017 *Captain Underpants*
2017 *Jumanji*
2018 *Untouchable*
2018 *Ride Along 3*

Chronology

1979 Kevin Hart is born in Philadelphia, Pennsylvania, on July 6

1997 Hart graduates from North East Philadelphia George Washington High School

2001 Hart receives role in *North Hollywood* pilot, which is cancelled before airing on television

2002 Hart debuts in film *Paper Soldiers* and in television show *Undeclared*

2003 Kevin and Torrei "Skipper" Hart get married

2005 Daughter Heaven Leigh Hart is born in March

2007 Hart's mother, Nancy, dies after long battle with ovarian cancer

2008 Son Hendrix Hart is born in November

2009 Hart's first album, *I'm a Grown Little Man*, is released

2010 *Seriously Funny* album is released

2011 Little Jumpman app is released; Kevin and Torrei divorce; *Laugh at My Pain* album is released

2012 Hart receives MVP honors in the NBA All-Star Celebrity Game; hosts MTV Video Music Awards

2013 *Real Husbands of Hollywood* premieres; Hart hosts *Saturday Night Live*; *Let Me Explain* DVD is released

Hart is arrested for driving under the influence

2014 Hart receives Teen Choice Award for Choice Movie Actor: Comedy, Nickelodeon Kids' Choice Favorite Funny Star Award, People's Comedy Star of the Year Award, and NAACP Image Award for Outstanding Comedy Series

2015 Hart hosts *Saturday Night Live*; receives MVP in NBA All-Star Celebrity Gme; receives MTV Comedic Genius Award; listed as number two in *Forbes*'s 2015 highest-paid celebrity ranking; receives NAACP Image Award for Outstanding Comedy Series

2016 California State Senate honors Hart with his own day, Kevin Hart Day, February 22; receives People's Choice Awards for Favorite Comedic Movie Actor and Favorite TV Cable Actor, and Shorty Award for the Best Comedian; hosts 2016 Oscars; Nike Free Train Instinct "Hart" training shoe is released; marries Eniko Parrish on August 16; *What Now?* DVD is released; listed number one in *Forbes*'s 2016 highest-paid-celebrity ranking; receives the 2,591st star on the Hollywood Walk of Fame

Chapter Notes

Chapter 1: Keeping It Real

1. Cynthia Fuchs, "Interview with Spike Lee and the Kings of Comedy," popmatters.com, http://www.popmatters.com/feature/kings-of-comedy/.

2. Luis Gomez, "Kevin Hart Not Shy about Past Flubs," *Chicago Tribune*, January 22, 2012, http://articles.chicagotribune.com/2012-01-22/entertainment/chi-interview-kevin-hart-chicago-20120122_1_kevin-hart-q-a-session-soul-plane.

3. Jonathan Landrum, "Kevin Hart Pokes Fun at His Life in Standup Movie," Backstage.com, September 9, 2012, http://www.backstage.com/news/kevin-hart-pokes-fun-at-his-life-in-standup-movie/.

4. Kevin Hart, *Laugh at My Pain*, directed by Leslie Small and Tim Story (Universal City, CA: Vivendi Entertainment, 2011). DVD.

5. Will Barlow, "Top Ten New York Comedy Writers Tell How to Start and Sustain a Career in Comedy," Indiewire.com, November 19, 2015, http://www.indiewire.com/2015/11/top-new-york-comedy-writers-tell-how-to-start-and-sustain-a-career-in-comedy-52182/.

6. Brad Wete, "Kevin Hart on How His Debut Indie Movie *Laugh at My Pain* Joked Its Way to a Top 10 Box Office Debut," *Entertainment*

Weekly, September 13, 2011, http://www.ew.com/
article/2011/09/13/kevin-hart-laugh-at-my-pain-
top-10-box-office.

7. Kevin Hart, YouTube, https://www.youtube.com/
watch?v=dwdTwjtVKOc.

Chapter 2: Finding Himself

1. Manuel McDonnell Smith, "Philadelphia's Rising
Star: Who's Laughing Now," *Urban Suburban*,
http://www.urbansuburbanmagazine.com/bestkept/
bestkept_Kevin-Hart.htm.

2. "Presidential Honor Award: Jim Ellis," International
Swimming Hall of Fame, http://www.ishof.org/jim-
ellis.html.

3. Eric Spitznagel, "Don't Be an A**hole, and Other
Life Lessons from Kevin Hart," *Men's Health*, March
6, 2015, http://www.menshealth.com/guy-wisdom/
life-lessons-from-kevin-hart.

4. Jonah Weiner, "Kevin Hart's Funny Business,"
Rolling Stone, July 29, 2015, http://www.
rollingstone.com/culture/features/kevin-harts-
funny-business-cover-story-20150729.

5. "Kevin Hart: How a Shoe Salesman Became an
$833 Million Movie Star," *Howard Stern Show*,
January 12, 2016, https://www.howardstern.com/
show/2016/1/12/kevin-hart-snl-bieber-ride-
along-2/.

6. Weiner, "Kevin Hart's Funny Business."

7. Amy Wallace, "Walking Tall with Kevin Hart,"
GQ.com, April 29, 2014, http://www.gq.com/story/
kevin-hart-funniest-people-may-2014.

8. Jessica Gross, "Kevin Hart: I Don't Need Therapy," *New York Times*, June 20, 2014, http://www.nytimes.com/2014/06/22/magazine/kevin-hart-i-dont-need-therapy.html?_r=1.

9. Cherri Greg, "A Re-birth of the Laff House Comedy Club in Philly?" CBS Philly, April 7, 2016, http://philadelphia.cbslocal.com/2016/04/07/a-re-birth-of-the-laff-house-comedy-club-in-philly/.

10. "Kevin Hart: How a Shoe Salesman Became an $833 Million Movie Star," *Howard Stern Show*.

11. Dave Itzkoff, "Life Sends Lemons: Make Comedy," *New York Times*, August 30, 2012, http://www.nytimes.com/2012/09/02/arts/television/kevin-hart-learns-to-tell-the-truth.html?pagewanted=all&_r=1.

12. Wallace, "Walking Tall with Kevin Hart."

13. Gross, "Kevin Hart: I Don't Need Therapy."

Chapter 3: Growing into "the" Little Man

1. Kevin Hart, *Laugh at My Pain*, directed by Leslie Small and Tim Story (Universal City, CA: Vivendi Entertainment, 2011). DVD.

2. "Kevin Hart: How a Shoe Salesman Became an $833 Million Movie Star," *Howard Stern Show*, January 12, 2016, https://www.howardstern.com/show/2016/1/12/kevin-hart-snl-bieber-ride-along-2/.

3. Tara Aquino, "Kevin Hart Talks *The Five-Year Engagement*, Judd Apatow, and Collaborating with Seth Rogen," Complex.com, April 24, 2012, http://

www.complex.com/pop-culture/2012/04/interview-kevin-hart-the-five-year-engagement.

4. Cal Fussman, "Kevin Hart: What I've Learned," *Esquire*, January 13, 2015, http://www.esquire.com/entertainment/interviews/a31020/kevin-hart-interview-0115/.

5. Luis Gomez, "Kevin Hart Not Shy about Past Flubs," *Chicago Tribune*, January 22, 2012, http://articles.chicagotribune.com/2012-01-22/entertainment/chi-interview-kevin-hart-chicago-20120122_1_kevin-hart-q-a-session-soul-plane.

6. Kevin Johnson, "Kevin Hart Says His *About Last Night* Character Is a First," *St. Louis Post Dispatch*, February 13, 2014, http://www.stltoday.com/entertainment/movies/kevin-hart-says-his-about-last-night-character-is-a/article_079fd482-c28a-54ad-a07a-d009413fde23.html.

7. Bobbie Whiteman, "I Messed Up My First Marriage!" Dailymail.com, October 11, 2016, http://www.dailymail.co.uk/tvshowbiz/article-3833206/Kevin-Hart-reveals-messed-marriage-young-22-tie-knot.html.

8. Eric Spitznagel, "Don't Be an A**hole, and Other Life Lessons from Kevin Hart," *Men's Health*, March 6, 2015, http://www.menshealth.com/guy-wisdom/life-lessons-from-kevin-hart.

9. Diana Ozemebhoya Eromosele, "Kevin Hart Says His Reaction to the Idea of His Son Being Gay Is about His Own Insecurities," theroot.com, August 3, 2015, http://www.theroot.com/blog/the

-grapevine/kevin_hart_describes_his_insecurities_
behind_his_reaction_if_his_son_was/.

Chapter 4: Doing Things the Kevin Hart Way

1. Brennan Williams, "Kevin Hart's *Laugh at My Pain* Marks Comedian's Big-Screen Stand-Up Debut," *Huffington Post*, September 9, 2011, http://www. huffingtonpost.com/2011/09/09/kevin-hart-laugh-at-my-pain_n_933927.html.

2. Dave Itzkoff, "Life Sends Lemons: Make Comedy," *New York Times*, August 30, 2012, http://www.nytimes.com/2012/09/02/arts/ television/kevin-hart-learns-to-tell-the-truth. html?pagewanted=all&_r=1.

3. Manuel McDonnell Smith, "Philadelphia's Rising Star: Who's Laughing Now," *Urban Suburban*, http://www.urbansuburbanmagazine.com/bestkept/ bestkept_Kevin-Hart.htm.

4. Jonathan Landrum, "Kevin Hart Pokes Fun at His Life in Standup Movie," *San Diego Union-Tribune*, September 9, 2011, http://www. sandiegouniontribune.com/sdut-kevin-hart-pokes-fun-at-his-life-in-standup-movie-2011sep09-story. html.

5. Ibid.

6. "Comedian Kevin Hart Launches His Own App," PR Newswire, April 12, 2011, http://www.prnewswire. com/news-releases/comedian-kevin-hart-launches-his-own-app-little-jumpman-for-iphone-ipad-and-ipod-touch-127583963.html.

7. "Kevin Hart to Host BET Awards," University Press International, May 18, 2011, http://www.upi.com/Kevin-Hart-to-host-BET-Awards/21511305745415/.

8. Eric Spitznagel, "Don't Be an A**hole, and Other Life Lessons from Kevin Hart," *Men's Health*, March 6, 2015, http://www.menshealth.com/guy-wisdom/life-lessons-from-kevin-hart.

9. Sydney Scott, "Torrei Hart Congratulates Ex Kevin Hart and Eniko Parrish on Getting Married," *Essence*, August 15, 2016, http://www.essence.com/2016/08/15/kevin-hart-eniko-parrish-married-torrei-hart-congratulates.

10. Cal Fussman, "Kevin Hart: What I've Learned," *Esquire*, January 13, 2015, http://www.esquire.com/entertainment/interviews/a31020/kevin-hart-interview-0115/.

11. JRKM, "Kevin Hart Gets Pitched, Talks Social Media at Just for Laughs," Pop Goes the News, July 28, 2016, https://popgoesthenews.com/author/johnnykcanada/.

12. Fussman, "Kevin Hart: What I've Learned."

Chapter 5: Kevin Explains Himself

1. Allison Samuels, "1940–2005: Richard Pryor," *Newsweek*, December 18, 2005, http://www.newsweek.com/1940-2005-richard-pryor-114071.

2. Ibid.

3. "Drake, Canada Win 2016 All-Star Celebrity Game," NBA.com, February 13, 2016, http://www.nba.com/news/as.celebrity.game/2016-celebrity-game-event-page/.

4. "Kevin Hart Speaks on Current Success, Politics, *The Five-Year Engagement* and More," UrbanBridgez.com, September 23, 2014, http://urbanbridgez.com/2014/09/23/ub-interview-kevin-hart-speaks-on-current-success-politics-the-five-year-engagement-more-2/.

5. Jonah Weiner, "Kevin Hart's Funny Business," *Rolling Stone*, July 29, 2015, http://www.rollingstone.com/culture/features/kevin-harts-funny-business-cover-story-20150729.

6. Dave Itzkoff, "Life Sends Lemons: Make Comedy," *New York Times*, August 30, 2012, http://www.nytimes.com/2012/09/02/arts/television/kevin-hart-learns-to-tell-the-truth.html?pagewanted=all&_r=1.

7. "What Does NAACP Stand For?" NAACP.org, http://www.naacp.org/about-us/.

8. Shalini Dore, "NAACP Image Awards: Kevin Hart Named Entertainer of the Year," *Variety*, February 22, 2014, http://variety.com/2014/film/awards/naacp-image-awards-kevin-hart-named-entertainer-of-the-year-12-years-a-slave-best-picture-1201116992/.

9. David Weiner, "Hart to Bieber: Everything Happens for a Reason," etonline.com, January 23, 2014, http://www.etonline.com/news/142820_Kevin_Hart_Reacts_to_Justin_Bieber_DUI/.

10. Lisa Schulz, "*The Wedding Ringer's* Kevin Hart on His Standing with Sony: 'It's All Good,'" *Variety*, January 8, 2015, http://variety.com/2015/scene/

vpage/the-wedding-ringers-kevin-hart-on-his-standing-with-sony-its-all-good-1201394904/.

11. "Kevin Hart Gives Computers to City Kids," NBC10.com, November 1, 2013, http://www.nbcphiladelphia.com/news/local/Kevin-Hart-Michael-Nutter-Computers-230182841.html.

12. David Henry, "Kevin Hart on Stolen Computers: I'll Be Back," 6ABC.com, November 17, 2013, http://6abc.com/archive/9362782/.

13. "Kevin Hart Gives Computers to City Kids."

14. Zayda Rivera, "Kevin Hart on DUI Arrest," *New York Daily News*, April 15, 2013, http://www.nydailynews.com/entertainment/gossip/kevin-hart-dui-arrest-drinking-driving-not-game-article-1.1317044.

15. Kevin Hart, Twitter post, April 14, 2013, 12:25 p.m., https://twitter.com/KevinHart4real/status/323517343147884544.

Chapter 6: "I Will Sleep When I Die"

1. Eric Spitznagel, "Don't Be an A**hole, and Other Life Lessons from Kevin Hart," *Men's Health*, March 6, 2015, http://www.menshealth.com/guy-wisdom/life-lessons-from-kevin-hart.

2. Ibid.

3. Jonah Weiner, "Kevin Hart's Funny Business," *Rolling Stone*, July 29, 2015, http://www.rollingstone.com/culture/features/kevin-harts-funny-business-cover-story-20150729.

4. Zach Seemayer, "Kevin Hart Says He and *Ride Along 2* Co-Star Ice Cube Are 'Best Friends

Forever,'" etonline.com, January 7, 2016, http://
www.etonline.com/movies/179483_kevin_hart_
says_he_and_ride_along_2_co_star_ice_cube_are_
best_friends_forever/.

5. Bob Strauss, "Kevin Hart Is Frank about the Adult
Version of *About Last Night*," *Los Angeles Daily News*,
February 13, 2014, http://www.dailynews.com/arts-
and-entertainment/20140213/kevin-hart-is-frank-
about-the-adult-version-of-about-last-night.

6. Oliver Gettell, "Kevin Hart, Regina Hall Spice Up
About Last Night, Reviews Say," *Los Angeles Times*,
February 14, 2014, http://articles.latimes.com/2014/
feb/14/entertainment/la-et-mn-about-last-night-
movie-reviews-critics-20140213.

7. Lisa Schulz, "*The Wedding Ringer*'s Kevin Hart on
His Standing with Sony: 'It's All Good,'" *Variety*,
January 8, 2015, http://variety.com/2015/scene/
vpage/the-wedding-ringers-kevin-hart-on-his-
standing-with-sony-its-all-good-1201394904/.

8. Jay Tiget, "Kevin Hart Talks *About Last Night*,
Being the 'It Guy,' and More," Indiewire.com,
February 13, 2014, http://www.indiewire.
com/2014/02/interview-kevin-hart-talks-about-
last-night-being-the-it-guy-and-more-opens-
tomorrow-161881/.

9. Michael Miller, "Kevin Hart Responds to
Accusation He Makes 'Stereotypical' Black Movies:
'I Make Movies for Everyone,'" *People*, January
28, 2016, http://people.com/movies/kevin-hart-
responds-to-accusation-he-makes-stereotypical-
movies/.

10. Weiner, "Kevin Hart's Funny Business."

11. Tiget, "Kevin Hart Talks *About Last Night*, Being the 'It Guy,' and More."

12. "35 and Ticking (2011)," coveringmedia.com, http://www.coveringmedia.com/movie/2011/05/35-and-ticking.html.

13. Ibid.

14. Alex Stedman, "Kevin Hart Responds to Sony 'Whore' Comment: 'I Protect My Brand,'" *Variety*, December 11, 2014, http://variety.com/2014/film/news/kevin-hart-responds-to-sony-whore-comments-i-protect-my-brand-1201377347/.

15. Michael Miller, "Kevin Hart Opens Up about His Painful Childhood and Forgiving His Ex-Drug Addict Dad," *People*, January 12, 2016, http://people.com/movies/kevin-hart-opens-up-about-his-painful-childhood-and-ex-drug-addict-dad/.

16. Kevin Hart, Twitter post, January 21, 2015, 2:40 p.m., https://twitter.com/kevinhart4real/status/558031462944219137.

17. Dorkys Ramos, "Kevin Hart to Offer Scholarships for United Negro College Fund," bet.com, April 13, 2015, http://www.bet.com/news/lifestyle/2015/04/13/kevin-hart-to-offer-scholarships-for-united-negro-college-fund.html.

18. Ibid.

19. HartBeat Productions, "Comedian Kevin Hart Donates Big to Children Battling Terminal Cancer," marketwired.com, September 2, 2014, http://www.marketwired.com/

press-release/comedian-kevin-hart-donates-big-to-children-battling-terminal-cancer-1973344.htm.

20. Nick Ramsey, "Will Ferrell and Kevin Hart Defend *Get Hard* from Criticism," msnbc.com, March 28, 2015, http://www.msnbc.com/the-last-word/will-ferrell-and-kevin-hart-defend-get-hard-criticism.

21. Ibid.

22. Steven Zeitchik, "For *Get Hard* Director, Race-Themed Satire Is a Tricky Enterprise," *Los Angeles Times*, March 26, 2015, http://www.latimes.com/entertainment/movies/moviesnow/la-et-mn-get-hard-kevin-hart-etan-cohen-comedy-race-20150326-story.html.

Chapter 7: Ready, Run, Action

1. Jonah Weiner, "Kevin Hart's Funny Business," *Rolling Stone*, July 29, 2015, http://www.rollingstone.com/culture/features/kevin-harts-funny-business-cover-story-20150729.

2. Ibid.

3. Brad Wete, "Kevin Hart on How His Debut Indie Movie *Laugh at My Pain* Joked Its Way to a Top 10 Box Office Debut," *Entertainment Weekly*, September 13, 2011, http://www.ew.com/article/2011/09/13/kevin-hart-laugh-at-my-pain-top-10-box-office.

4. Rally Staff, "Guess What Crazy Thing Kevin Hart Did Last Weekend?" Rally Health, June 8, 2015, https://www.rallyhealth.com/guess-what-crazy-thing-kevin-hart-did-this-weekend/.

5. Lambeth Hochwald, "Comedian Kevin Hart Really Does 1,000 Sit-Ups Every Day," *Parade*, August 1, 2016, http://parade.com/496170/lhochwald/comedian-kevin-hart-even-does-knee-lifts-during-interviews/.

6. Gerald Flores, "Keeping Up with Kevin Hart: Nike's Biggest Spokesperson," solecollector.com, June 7, 2016, http://solecollector.com/news/2016/06/kevin-hart-interview.

7. Rally Staff, "Rally Health Teams Up with Kevin Hart," Rally Health, April 23, 2015, https://www.rallyhealth.com/rally-and-kevin-hart-to-laugh-themselves-to-health/.

8. Ibid.

9. Kirsten Fleming, "Why Thousands of People Are Running with Kevin Hart," *New York Post*, October 27, 2015, http://nypost.com/2015/10/27/why-thousands-of-people-are-running-with-kevin-hart/.

10. Flores, "Keeping Up with Kevin Hart: Nike's Biggest Spokesperson."

11. Drew Mackie, "Kevin Hart to be Honored at MTV Movie Awards," *People*, March 30, 2015, http://people.com/tv/kevin-hart-to-receive-comedic-genius-award-at-2015-mtv-movie-awards/.

12. Kevin Hart, "God Is Truly Amazing . . .," Instagram post, July 29, 2015, https://www.instagram.com/p/5ujz9LCYkl/.

Chapter 8: All Grown Up Now

1. "An Introduction to the Shorty Awards," Shorty Awards, http://shortyawards.com/about.

2. "Sen. Hall Welcomes Kevin Hart to the California State Senate," YouTube video, posted by California State Democrats, February 23, 2016, https://www.youtube.com/watch?v=SAi3QNB1B78.

3. Kevin Hart, Twitter post, February 22, 2016, 6:36 p.m., https://twitter.com/KevinHart4real.

4. Arlene Washington, "Kevin Hart, Dwayne Johnson Talk Their 'Brotherly Chemistry' at *Central Intelligence* Premiere," *Hollywood Reporter*, June 11, 2016, http://www.hollywoodreporter.com/news/kevin-hart-dwayne-johnson-talk-901828.

5. Amanda Keegan, "Kevin Hart, Dwayne Johnson Surprise Kids with Anti-Bullying Message," abcnews.go.com, June 15, 2016, http://abcnews.go.com/Entertainment/kevin-hart-dwayne-johnson-surprise-kids-anti-bullying/story?id=39761760.

6. "Kevin Hart on Being Robbed over the Weekend," interview by Steve Harvey, July 2016, http://news.iheart.com/onair/steve-harvey-morning-show-55813/kevin-hart-on-being-robbed-over-14822107/.

7. Jackie Willis, "Kevin Hart Shares Image of Man He Says Robbed His House—But It's Actually a Stock Photo," etonline.com, June 22, 2016, http://www.etonline.com/news/191650_kevin_hart_shares_image_of_the_man_he_says_robbed_his_house_but_it_actually_a_stock_photo/.

8. Lambeth Hochwald, "Comedian Kevin Hart Really Does 1,000 Sit-Ups Every Day," *Parade*, August 1, 2016, http://parade.com/496170/lhochwald/

comedian-kevin-hart-even-does-knee-lifts-during-interviews/.

9. "Kevin Hart Thinks Cats Are Evil," YouTube video, posted by Kids Flix, July 13, 2016, https://www.youtube.com/watch?v=ajYj0zEekU4.

10. Chanelle Harbin, "Kevin Hart Addresses Diversity at Oscars 2016," oscars.go.com, February 29, 2016, http://oscar.go.com/news/oscar-news/kevin-hart-addresses-diversity-at-oscars-2016.

11. Leah Greenblatt, "Kevin Hart on Diversity in Hollywood: 'Let's Get to a Place Where Everybody Can Succeed," *Entertainment Weekly*, August 5, 2016, http://www.ew.com/article/2016/08/05/kevin-hart-diversity-hollywood-oscars-so-white.

12. Stefan Kyriazis, "*Secret Life of Pets* Kevin Hart: I'll Fight Racism and Win an Oscar Playing a White Bunny," June 24, 2016, *Daily Express*, http://www.express.co.uk/entertainment/films/683173/Kevin-Hart-Secret-Life-of-Pets-Oscars-So-white-Hollywood-racism.

13. Gerald Flores, "Keeping Up with Kevin Hart: Nike's Biggest Spokesperson," solecollector.com, June 7, 2016, http://solecollector.com/news/2016/06/kevin-hart-interview.

14. Barry Janoff, "NBA's Draymond Green Find Kevin Hart Is Friend and Footlocker (Fashion) Faux," February 3, 2016, nysportsjournalism.com, http://www.nysportsjournalism.com/kevin-hart-is-foot-locker-faux/.

15. Meena Jang, "Kevin Hart Talks Working with Dwayne Johnson, Shares Advice for Aspiring

Comedians: 'Don't Be a Talker, Be a Doer,'" *Hollywood Reporter*, July 8, 2016, http://www. hollywoodreporter.com/news/kevin-hart-talks-working-dwayne-909475.

16. Roast (comedy), Wikipedia, https://en.wikipedia. org/wiki/Roast_(comedy).

17. Michael Miller, "Kevin Hart Opens Up about His Painful Childhood and Forgiving His Ex-Drug Addict Dad," *People*, January 12, 2016, http:// people.com/movies/kevin-hart-opens-up-about-his-painful-childhood-and-ex-drug-addict-dad/.

18. Naja Rayne, "Kevin Hart Reveals His Son Hendrix Will Serve as His Best Man," *People*, January 14, 2016, http://people.com/celebrity/kevin-hart-reveals-his-son-hendrix-will-serve-as-his-best-man/.

19. Dave Itzkoff, "Life Sends Lemons: Make Comedy," *New York Times*, August 30, 2012, http://www.nytimes.com/2012/09/02/arts/television/kevin-hart-learns-to-tell-the-truth. html?pagewanted=all&_r=1.

20. Renee Grant, "Philly's Kevin Hart Awarded Star on Hollywood Walk of Fame," wogl.cbslocal. com, October 14, 2016, http://wogl.cbslocal. com/2016/10/14/phillys-kevin-hart-awarded-star-on-hollywood-walk-of-fame/.

Chapter 9: What Next?

1. Nardine Saad, "The Jokes, Folks: Justin Bieber's Roasters Get a Walloping of Their Own," *Los Angeles Times*, March 31, 2015, http://www.latimes. com/entertainment/tv/showtracker/la-et-st-justin-

bieber-roast-jokes-kevin-hart-shaq-snoop-martha-stewart-20150330-story.html.

2. Eric Spitznagel, "Don't Be an A**hole, and Other Life Lessons from Kevin Hart," *Men's Health*, March 6, 2015, http://www.menshealth.com/guy-wisdom/life-lessons-from-kevin-hart.

3. Richard Zoglin, "Stand-up Comedy," *Encyclopædia Britannica*, May 12, 2016, https://www.britannica.com/art/stand-up-comedy.

4. Mike Tyrkus, "Interview with Kevin Hart and Regina Hall, the Co-Stars of *About Last Night*," Cinemanerdz.com, February 17, 2014, http://cinemanerdz.com/interview-with-kevin-hart-and-regina-hall-the-co-stars-of-about-last-night/.

5. Internet Movie Database, Kevin Hart, imdb.com, http://www.imdb.com/name/nm0366389/.

6. Jonah Weiner, "Kevin Hart's Funny Business," *Rolling Stone*, July 29, 2015, http://www.rollingstone.com/culture/features/kevin-harts-funny-business-cover-story-20150729.

Glossary

A-list A group of people or things of the highest excellence, eminence, or social importance.

antic Moment of ludicrous or other unusual behavior.

biopic A biographical motion picture.

booking agent A person who arranges events for performers.

debut A first public appearance in a film or television series.

imprint A name under which publishers issue books.

improvise To compose, recite, or sing on the spur of the moment; "improv" is a show in which comedians make up jokes as they go.

method actor An actor who uses techniques to closely identify with the character he or she is portraying.

mixtape A group of favorite pieces of music, typically by different artists, recorded onto a cassette tape or other medium.

newbie A person who has recently started a particular activity.

persona A character in fiction, such as in a film or television show.

playbill Advertisement for a film that usually announces the cast.

pyrotechnics A display of fireworks used for signals.

seasoned Performing for a long time and experienced.

spin-off A television show starring a character or subject matter that was popular in an earlier show.

talent scout A person who discovers and recruits people of talent for a specialized field.

theatrics Staged effects for performance.

uncredited Not receiving credits for appearing in a movie or television show; also referred to as "unbilled."

Further Reading

Books

Berry, S. Torriano, and Venise T. Berry. *Historical Dictionary of African American Cinema*, 2nd ed. Lanham, MD: Rowman & Littlefield Publishers, 2015.

Hart, Kevin. *From the Hart*. New York, NY: 37 INK, 2017.

Smith, Emily. *Kevin Hart Handbook*. Queensland, Australia: Emereo Publishing, 2013.

Tafoya, Eddie. *Icons of African American Comedy*. Santa Barbara, CA: Greenwood, 2011.

Websites

Kevin Hart

http://kevinhartnation.com

Kevin Hart's official website

Kevin Hart Awards

http://www.imdb.com/name/nm0366389/awards

IMDb's list of awards won by Kevin Hart

Movies

Jumanji. Dir. Jake Kasdan. Columbia Pictures, 2017.

The Secret Life of Pets. Dir. Chris Renaud and Yarrow Cheney. Universal Pictures, 2016.

Index